Indo-US Relations and Peace Prospects in South West Indian Ocean

Indo-US Relations and Peace Prospects in South West Indian Ocean

Amita Agarwal

2008
Kaveri Books
New Delhi - 110 002

First Published in 2008

ISBN-10 : 81-7479-083-7
ISBN-13 : 978-81-7479-083-5

Published by
Kaveri Books
4697/ 5-21 A, Ansari Road,
New Delhi - 110 002 (India).
Ph.: 011-2328 8140, 2324 5799
E-mail: kaveribooks@vsnl.com

Laser Typesetting by
Aarati Computers, Delhi - 110 009.

Printed at
Chawla Offset Printers, Delhi-110 052.

PRINTED IN INDIA

Preface

Water is essential both to the creation and sustenance of life. Without the oceans human civilization could not exist. We have always taken the oceans as a permanent feature, their resources as inexhaustible that cannot be depleted however much we make their use as well as misuse. This elixir of life is taken as an integral part of life, which does not require any regulation or looking after let alone development, cultivation and conservation for future generations. This uncalled for notion has taken deep roots in our psyche because the oceans have existed from the very creation of life and thus they are taken for granted. They have been there since the very creation of the earth and will remain long after we are gone. The same cannot be said about their resources that are being rapidly used and depleted.

Maritime resources have always played a very significant role in human development. The oceans have been used since time immemorial for fishing and as a highway for ships in peace and in war. Due to permanent visibility of oceans they were once considered a **'Common Heritage of Mankind'**. This perception developed largely due to certain beliefs e.g.,

1. Fishing stocks were considered inexhaustible.
2. Navigation was taken as concerning only the surface of the seas.
3. Any danger of serious impairment of the seas as a result of human activities was not expected.
4. It was believed that navigation beyond a narrow coastal belt is totally subject to national jurisdiction and requires no regulation, and
5. It was believed that open space is so vast and its potential uses so limited that there is virtually no danger of any serious conflict over the use of the oceans among the sovereign nations.

But in contemporary times the situation has completely changed. Uses of the seas have increased manifold and so has the belief that maritime resources are not inexhaustible and need to be protected, developed and conserved for future generations. With this realization the possibility of conflicts among sovereign nations over the use of maritime resources has also increased manifold.

From the recent developments it has become quite evident that the uses of the oceans today are very different in nature and intensity from what they used to be a few years ago. This situation is rapidly changing by the day due to the innovations and development of science and technology. The oceans in all their dimensions are increasingly being penetrated, used and exploited for a variety of *nouvelle* purposes. Gradually but visibly the oceans are fast becoming part of man's living space and the hub of activity. We are witnessing a silent revolution in our perception of maritime environment. Certain factors have brought the importance of the oceans to the forefront. A few examples are worth mentioning here;

1. Now it has become an accepted fact that, at least, the living resources of the oceans are not inexhaustible. So, they are not only to be used in a cautious and planned manner but also to be conserved and developed for the use of our future generations. This becomes imperative specially because we have already seen the results of unplanned use of the scarce land resources that are on the verge of extinction. Maritime resources, which are the only hope of humankind are not only more scarce than the land resources but are also much more expensive and require far more advanced technology for their economic harvest.
2. Increasing size of vessels of war and peace as well as density of traffic in congested areas has made the regulation of navigation mandatory.
3. Visible contamination of the seas has not only become a threat to the living resources of the oceans and human security of all those who consume these but also has activated environmental activists. These groups are trying to draw the attention of all concerned and put some sense in the policy - makers for ensuring human security, specially in the coastal areas. Due to large scale pollution in the coastal area, the tourist industry of some coastal

states has already been adversely affected that in turn is having a negative impact on their economies to a great extent.

4. Development of science and technology has opened new vistas for harvesting the ocean's non-living resources, resulting in the probability of their unplanned use. The use of non-living resources like living resources has to be planned and regulated for the optimum use of maritime resources and simultaneous cultivation for the use of future generations.

5. It has been conceded that some areas, such as the sea bed beyond national jurisdiction, and new uses of the seas such as artificial islands, floating and fixed installations and sea bed habitats may require detailed regulation and deviation from the principle of freedom of the high seas in regard to the interests of other states.

6. Growing traffic in drugs and human beings, sea piracy, terrorist activities and proliferation of nuclear arms in and around the oceans have become greater causes of concern, and all these problems demand immediate attention and solution if peace and stability is to be maintained.

7. Increasing awareness of maritime resources and their importance for national development and maintenance of national integrity and sovereignty has made even traditionally non-maritime powers like China and Japan to concentrate on development, modernization and deployment of their navies in various parts of oceans which were earlier totally ignored.

8. Disintegration of the Soviet Union and increasing trends of liberalization, privatization and globalization have thrown open new areas of cooperation as well as interference in the name of trade and commerce. The world oceans cannot be expected to remain unaffected by these trends.

9. Emergence of the United States of America as a single super power and its high - handed policies in West Asia and other parts of the world also are causes of concern for peace - loving nations of the world.

10. The non effective role played by the United Nations in various crises as in Kuwait, Iraq, Afghanistan and Kosovo has not been

a help in any way to the cause of world peace, let alone peace in the Indian Ocean.

All this is enough indication not only of the growing importance of the oceans for the very survival of the entire human kind but of the dangers for peace and human security. The Indian Ocean is no exception to all these worrying trends. Rather due to its geo-strategic importance threats to peace in the region increase manifold. The situation is not helped by the entry of traditionally non maritime powers like China and Japan in the ocean surrounded by all the major religions of the world. Thus the region becomes more susceptible to conflicts between and among the hostile powers.

The small, politically unstable and economically developing states of this region of turmoil are an easy prey to the designs of stronger nations due to their mutual suspicions which make them seek outside help in any emergency. Aided by the growing trends of liberalization, privatization and globalization, these countries have become an easy prey to big power rivalry in the name of trade and commerce.

The absence of a powerful regional navy that can control and protect interests of the regional countries, rapid development, modernization and deployment of extra-regional navies in the region lead one to say that the Indian ocean is not likely to be an area notable for its peace and stability in the near future.

The basic purpose of this study is to look into the challenges and prospects of peace in the Indian Ocean region with special reference to the Indo-US naval relations and policies and practices of other South Asian countries.

Contents

1

Introduction

The Indian Ocean covering only about 20 per cent of the world's ocean area has consistently occupied a position of preeminence unrivalled by the Pacific or Atlantic Ocean. The ocean has always figured prominently not only in the lives of the people in the littoral countries but also of the people of distant lands. The geopolitical prominence of the Ocean of the *Pre-Gaman era* was intimately connected with the *fabulous riches and spices* of the Indies.[1]The spice trade with the East, "one of the great motivating factors of history"[2] and one which yielded the largest profits to merchants as these commodities were universal in demand, could only be conducted across the Indian Ocean, making its waters so much more important. *The importance of spices in times past is probably surpassed only by the present-day prominence of oil.*[3] The importance of the ocean in providing access to the ports of India can be gauged from the fact that *Gama's arrival* at Calicut was labeled as *"the realization of a 200 year old dream."*[4] In an age when pepper was "ranked with precious stones" the importance of the ocean providing access to the spices could well be understood.

Vasco Da Gama, when he arrived in India and heralded four and a half centuries of European hegemony, had said that it was his task to find "*Christians* and *spices*". No less significant were the famous words of a later Sixteenth Century Portuguese navigator *Alfonso d' Albuquerque*, who spoke of ***"The Three Keys"*** *to the Indian Ocean*, The Straits of Malacca and Singapore in the East, the strait of Hormuz at the entrance to the Persian Gulf and the straits of the Red Sea and Aden in the West. Although changes in weapons and military technology have altered the methods of warfare and structure of power since the Sixteenth Century, the geographical factors have remained of supreme strategic importance. The trends were witnessed by the disposition of British naval forces later on and, in more recent times, by the ever growing presence of regional and extra-regional navies i.e. Indian, Chinese, Indonesian, French and Pakistani to name of a few.

The Indian Ocean has become an area of immense importance in the recent past. This change has been brought about by two vital factors: first, the gradual withdrawal of the British Royal Navy from the East of Suez, which coincided with the formulation of British Indian Ocean Territory (BIOT) and second, the related appearance of a new naval power i.e. the Soviet Union. Prior to these developments this area was ignored in comparison to the Pacific and Atlantic Ocean regions.

The outstanding feature of the politics of the Indian Ocean is that no single littoral country has ever exercised exclusive control over this strategically as well as economically important area. Earlier, the politics of these regions was dominated by the European powers having the aim to control the spice trade and later on to control the oil. But, it is significant that this trade was carried between Europe and the littoral nations; intra-regional trade was but nominal, in comparison to that the basic trading patterns are still overwhelmingly external rather than intra-regional.

It is countries beyond the shores of the Indian Ocean that consume India's products and the littoral countries cannot be said to form a distinct Indian Ocean economy in the sense that North American and Western Europe form an Atlantic economy.

The strategic importance of the region first came to the forefront due to some new developments on the international platform i.e. the Bangladesh liberation war of 1971 and oil embargo by the Middle East Countries in 1973-74. The Iranian revolution and its aftermath and the seizure of the Great Mosque in Mecca are two other reminders of the precariousness of oil supply to the oil-starved countries.

Along the Western Indian Ocean in the Horn of Africa and South Africa, the forces of nationalism, liberation and racism continue to vie for influence and ascendancy against the background of vast income disparities and the need for economic development. The invasion of Afghanistan by the erstwhile Soviet Union had again drawn world attention to the region. On the other hand the United States' efforts to convert Diego Garcia into a major naval base and the strong opposition by the Govt. of Mauritius which put forward its claims on the island time and again aroused suspicions in the international community. With all these developments, it is little wonder that this area is often described as *an arch of instability*.

The countries that have freed themselves from the western powers have had their role in world politics substantially increased as a result of the changed world balance of forces in favour of national liberation, overcoming the bitter resistance of the western powers, beating off the attacks of neo-colonialism and strengthening their political and economic independence. As most of these countries of the third world are either the littoral or hinterland countries of the Indian Ocean they have mobilized themselves into forming an Indian Ocean Community to protect their interests. This feeling has become stronger by the day as the importance of the oceans has started coming up front. These countries are no longer an object but a subject of history. A special place among these countries is held by India, whose policy has been exerting a marked positive influence on the course of events in present-day life and which has also established itself as an important maritime state.

There are many factors which make India a major and influential force of the region e.g. peaceable foreign policy, growing economic might, important geographical location, considerable size of its territory and population, vast coastal areas and a EEZ, its scientific development, newly achieved nuclear power status and finally its policy of non-alignment. Being leader of over a hundred non-aligned nations, India had acquired a say in international forums which is now supported by its recently acquired nuclear power status.

Though littoral States are facing all sorts of difficulties in demilitarization and arms control in such a vital region, their efforts are earnest and honest. Despite the strong desire of the littoral states to insulate themselves from the cold war, modern communications make it unrealistic for them to exclude the great powers from the area. Despite all these difficulties the littoral nations, including India, have been doing their best so that this area may be declared a zone of peace / nuclear weapon free zone so that the countries of the Indian Ocean Region can concentrate on their development without any misgivings.

It is said that the Indian Ocean is not likely to be an area notable for its peace and stability; on the contrary, pressures of population, the demand for scarce natural resources, racial and frontier disputes together with weakness of most of the littoral governments due to their newness, are likely to make their contribution to instability. New threats to the security of this region have developed (in addition to the traditional ones) like drug trafficking, smuggling, human smuggling, piracy, terrorism and pollution of marine environment.

Geographical Features

Slightly more than 70 per cent of the earth's surface lies under 330 million cubic miles (1,375 million cubic km) of ocean. It is a volume of water sufficient to cover the globe to a depth of 12,000 feet (3,660 metres) if the surface of the planet were smooth. Salt water covers about 60 per cent of the Northern Hemisphere and about 81 per cent of the Southern Hemisphere.

Although the World Ocean is global i.e. everywhere continuous, it was discovered piecemeal and its various parts were given different names at different times. The Pacific Ocean was known as the Western Ocean, the Atlantic as the Great Ocean and the North Atlantic as the North Ocean. **The names Atlantic, Pacific, Indian, Arctic and Antarctic were recommended by the Royal Geographical Society of London in 1845.**[5]

The Indian Ocean is the only ocean of the world, which is known after the name of one of its littoral countries. It is the third largest ocean of the world, after the Pacific and Atlantic Oceans.[6] It extends over only 30 million square miles while the Pacific Ocean covers 60 million and the Atlantic Ocean (without the Arctic Region) covers only 34 million square miles. In its more usual narrower meaning the Indian Ocean covers only 16 million square miles[7].

The Indian Ocean situated between the two big oceans and providing a link between them enjoys great strategic significance in the maritime affairs of the world. The **cartographic definition of the Indian Ocean,** accepted by the United Nations, is as follows:

(a) the dividing line between the Atlantic and Indian Ocean is the Meridian of Cape Agulhas (20°0′E),

(b) the dividing line between the Pacific and Indian Ocean is the Meridian of the South-East Cape of Tasmania (147°0′ E),

(c) the dividing line between the Atlantic Ocean and the Indian Ocean is the 60°0′ South Latitude, and

(d) the northern limits of the Indian Ocean are well defined by the continent of Asia.

The maximum length of the Indian Ocean is over 10,460 kms. (North to South) and its breadth is nearly 9,635 kms. (East to West). It covers nearly 20.6 per cent of the total oceanic area of the world. Its average depth is about 3643 metres and its maximum known depth is 7,393 metres at "Wharton Deep" near the island of Sumatra.[8]

Indian Ocean as a Region

As the Indian Ocean has continuously been gaining importance and the countries of the Indian Ocean region have become aware of its importance, some scholars/ nations have started challenging the very idea of establishment of peace zone in this region on nefarious grounds. They are not ready to accept the area even as a region so that all demands of its being declared a zone of peace (and its implementation) can be thwarted. Some western studies raise the doubt of whether it is a region in terms of global policies.

Authors like Barry Buzan outright reject the case for the Indian Ocean being a region.[9] He observed that as things stand, the attempt to conjure up an Indian Ocean Region tends to detract more from understanding than it adds. The problems of omission and superficiality which arise from the scale and diversity of the area, are not offset by the weak and tentative linkage which the Indian Ocean framework provides.[10] A US study also reached the same conclusions stating that the Indian Ocean region lacks common religion, political, economic and ethnic traditions, with bitter divisions and diverse local interests and is vulnerable to disruption from within and without.[11] An Australian scholar T.B. Miller remarked, **"there is no such thing as the Indian Ocean (Region), except as a cartographic expression. It has no coherence, no unity, economically, culturally, politically and strategically."**[12]

These studies raise two fundamental questions. What is a region in international politics? And what are the pre-requisites for an area to be considered as a region?

If the definitions available are analysed it is stated that, "In international sphere, a region may consist of a group of nation states possessing a common culture, common political interests and often a formal organization."[13] It has also been observed that, "A region is invariably an area embracing the territories of three or more states. These states are bound together by ties of common interests as well as geography. They are not necessarily contiguous, or even in the same continent."[14]

Scholars like F.A. Vali, on the other hand, consider this area as a region. Vali observed that for geographic and geostrategic reasons the Indian Ocean region should be treated as one unit, in spite of divergent-ethnic, cultural and economic considerations, interrelations between history, geography and strategic reasons are here more solid, more forcible and more conscious than most other parts of the world.[15]

An analysis[16] of the region on the basis of the four criteria - geographic, politico-strategic, economic and social would be relevant at this stage.

(1) **Geographically**, the Indian Ocean represents the states, which are almost contiguous in a ring shape. Except Australia, all other states form part of Asia (25 states) and Africa (21 states). These 36 littoral and 11 hinterland states are well connected with each other through easy communication links via sea or land and air routes.

(2) **In political and strategic** terms, both from the "external perspectives of the various powers and the internal perspectives" visualised by the Indian Ocean states, the Indian Ocean stands out to be a single unit or a region. All the external powers, for their policy decisions, have treated the area as one region. Littoral States too have many common values, common experiences and common aims and ideals, which are evident from their demand of a peace zone for the region. The fact is reiterated by establishment of IOR - ARC.

(3) At first glance homogeneity of **economic** conditions of the Indian Ocean states is not readily apparent but, if observed closely, it is found that most of the countries have narrow - based economies, highly vulnerable to the vicissitudes of the global economic system. Their economic conditions provide a unity in two forms: first, in the form of protest against the existing international economic system, and, second, for an effort towards more and more regional cooperation to preserve their independence and look after welfare of their masses.

Out of 47 countries, with the exception of only six-India, South Africa, Singapore, Pakistan, Australia and Indonesia

- all are non-industrial states having narrow - based economies. They have to face severe economic challenges in terms of the prevalent global economic system. All the states of the area face similar problems, have similar interests and aspire for similar objectives in the international system.

(4) **Socially** the three main factors that provide unity to this area are religion, culture and racial intercourse among the Indian Ocean states. Despite divergent religious sentiments in different states each prevalent religion has influenced the region to a great extent. The main religions which influence these states are-Islam, Hinduism, Buddhism and Christianity.

Cultural linkages between the Indian Ocean states are varied and very old, and racial intercourse between the different peoples of this region is another linkage of unity in this area. Racial intercourse too is not unheard of in the region among the different races of the region. The trend has been strengthened due to easy mobility within resulting in large number's of indigenous diaspora in all the countries.

This analysis proves that the area fulfils all the requisites to be termed a region. Non-alignment and the demand for implementation of peace zone also provide an enhanced, distinct identity to this region.

Divisions of the Indian Ocean Region

In a study by the Australian Department of Foreign Affairs the following divisions of the Indian Ocean area were suggested:

(1) East Africa and the Ocean region east of it;

(2) The Northwest from Somalia around to Iran including the Red Sea. The gulf of Aden and the Persian Gulf;

(3) The Asian Subcontinent and the Sea South-West, and

(4) Southwest Asia and Australia.

An Indian Scholar divided the region into four pivotal areas:

i) South Africa

ii) South-West Asia

iii) India and Pakistan, and

iv) South-East Asia and Australia.[17]

These two schemes are basically similar except that the Australian version is more precise and comprehensive.[18] But, any scheme of divisions of the Indian Ocean region should not be viewed as watertight compartments; on the contrary, trends, policies and interests between neighbouring subregions frequently overlap. International relations are too complex to be confined to certain predetermined areas without allowing for their impact on neighbouring or even more distant nations. The geographic fact of being located along or near the shores of one ocean increases the interrelationships that manifest themselves in tangible and intangible ways. The geographic vicinity creates stronger impulses between the nations thus involved but in certain situations the impulse affects even more distant yet geographically still close communities. The ultimate truth has been poignantly expressed by the leader of an Indian Ocean nation, "The importance of a universal intercontinental understanding and association is in no way diminished by the assertion that geography continues to remain the most important single factor in the formulation of a country's Foreign Policy".[19]

Whether the Indian Ocean is a geographical unit or not, to make it clear, we have to discuss what a geographical unit means:

Geographers operate with the concept of a geographic region, although they more often disagree than agree as to the characteristics or requirements of an area to be considered as such. The French expression *compage*, also used by English speaking geographers, to whom it means, "frame work" or "structure" is even more to the point. The *compage* is an area interrelated by natural and societal features relevant for a specific consideration or study characteristic of a geographic region overlapping into other neighbouring regions. Therefore, there exists no "total region" i.e. one which has features not shared with other regions. Geographic regions may differ in size; they may even extend to a large sphere of continental dimensions. From the point of view of the student of a region, what matters is that in addition to similar features its differing characteristics should be amenable to assimilation. Ultimately, we should keep in mind Richard Hartshoren's advice, that a regional division is not true picture of reality, but it is an arbitrary device of the student depending on what elements appear to him as most significant. It should also be remembered that "region is a term of art not science, and regions in world politics emerge only because policy-makers find within a given territorial area a number of international problems that are discrete".[20]

True, there is no ethnic, cultural or religious unity in the area but it should also be remembered that the region couldn't be clearly divided on ethnic, cultural and religious grounds. However what is not so well known is that despite wide differences among these societies they have certain marked unifying traits as well. Economically they are still undergoing the ordeals of change from underdeveloped to developing states. An evidence of their common strain of culture was provided by the non-aligned meet in New Delhi in 1983.[21]

Indeed, ethno-religious differences do divide the population of the Indian Ocean region. However most of the sea is simultaneously tied together by followers of the same faith, culture and often also·language. There is diversity but amidst the diversity there is unity. And why should one talk about only the Indian Ocean in this context? Any one trend, religion or ethnic group can exclusively dominate no region. There have to be many different groups present in a region in the multidimensional world of today.

Jacques Auber has projected concepts of not one but two Indian Ocean regions; one which he called the "World of Cancer", north of the equator on both sides of the Tropic of Cancer. The other, the "World of Capricorn" South of the equator, parallel to the Tropic of Capricorn. The first world is the home of three major civilizations i.e. Islam, Hinduism and Buddhism. The second is less inhabited, mostly by immigrant populations, who came from various parts of the world. Evidently, this division did not take care of the cross-cultural and religious currents, which prevail throughout the area.[22]

Though western writers do raise doubts about the geopolitical unity of the Indian Ocean Region, the noted Indian Scholar K.M. Panikkar, emphasising its geographical unity writes, "Its geographical structure is such as being walled off on three sides by land, with the southern side of Asia framing a roof over it". But the vital mark - according to him - which differentiates the region from the two other oceans is "not the two sides but the subcontinent of India which juts out far into the sea for a thousand miles to its tapering end at Cape Comorin. He concludes that despite the vastness of its surface and oceanic characters, the Indian Ocean has "some of the features of a land locked sea"[23].

The geographical significance of the specific physical features of the Indian Ocean can only be fully appreciated when viewed from the perspective of its historical precedents.

Historical Legacy

Before the Portuguese arrived, the Indian Ocean area was almost totally fragmented. Only the Islamic West was connected with the Malay-Indonesian east. But the Islamic link created only a religious-cultural identity with no politico-military content.

In contrast, the Portuguese invasion was purely military and political, though at times it was strongly opposed; it is no exaggeration to assert that despite its short comings Portugal was able to establish a *thalassocracy*, a naval empire, within the Indian Ocean, lasting for about a century.

In the late sixteenth and early seventeenth centuries, the Dutch barred from the Lisbon market entered the Indian Ocean to procure pepper and spices from their very source. Whereas the Portuguese had planned an imperium in Asia, the Dutch were prompted by purely commercial motives and their operations were conducted by an East India Company, the first of its kind.[24]

The Portuguese monocracy was challenged and destroyed by the Dutch and the English. The interregnum that followed was characterized by the struggle among the Dutch, English and French for the succession to Portugal's trade monopoly. Eventually, the struggle developed into a prolonged duel between Britain and France. This rivalry turned into a scramble not only for trade but also for land. The Indian subcontinent and most of the coastland of the Ocean fell to Britain.[25]

The British Policy in the region was based on three fundamental conceptions:

(1) that no other great power should be able to establish, on the Indian Ocean, bases and ports having secured land and air communications with its own main base;

(2) the control by British Sea and air power of the naval gateways into the Indian Ocean; and

(3) the maintenance in India, the geographical key stone of the whole region, of a strategic reserve for the defence of India herself and other parts of the Indian Ocean.[26]

During nearly one century and a half Britain succeeded in turning the Indian Ocean into a Virtual British Lake. Unlike the Portuguese control which consisted of occupation of scattered points along the coast, British Sovereignty extended over most of the land surrounding the ocean. The region thus had unification much more perfect and durable than that of Lisbon. Nobody would have denied the "oneness" of the region as a geopolitical or strategic entity.[27]

In the post World War II period the Indian Ocean has again become politically fragmented.

Is this another interregnum? Hardly so, it seems rather unlikely that any power, Super power or littoral power would be able or even willing to establish hegemony or near hegemony over the region as whole. In other words, an Indian Ocean Empire, like that of the British, is now past history, whether the alleged vacuum, in terms of naval power, will be filled in by a non-regional thalassocratic power depends on many contingencies. During the cold war era, both within and outside the region, there were fears that super power rivalry might draw the area into a series of conflagrations, as the Anglo-French rivalry caused in India and in the waters leading to it. Since the end of the cold war the situation has become worse. Now instead of rivalry between just the two super powers i.e. the USA and the former USSR many other actors have joined the race to control or influence the Indian Ocean. China, France, Japan and Indonesia are a few to name in addition to India and Pakistan. Hence the movement for denuclearization or neutralization of the region.[28]

Geo-strategic Importance of the Indian Ocean

Strategically the Indian Ocean occupies a unique position. This is the only ocean in the world which is hemmed in the North by the Inner or marginal crescent of the "Heartland of Mackinder" and as such is on the South of the "World Island". It not only washes the shores of Southern and Western Australia; South-East, South and West Asia; East and South Africa, but also provides these lands with an easy route for transportation to the Pacific Coast countries in the East and to the Mediterranean and the Atlantic Ocean region in the West. In the North the Indian Peninsula penetrates Southwards into the northern periphery of the Indian Ocean to divide it into two water bodies, known as the Bay of Bengal and the Arabian Sea, which lies with the East and the West of the Peninsula respectively, thus offering the countries bordering on these indentations a maritime location. From the Arabian Sea, vessels can sail up to the Black Sea and the Sea of Azor in the former Soviet Union through the Red Sea, the Suez canal the Mediterranean Sea, the Aegean Sea, the Strait of Dardanelles, the Sea of Marmara and the Strait of Bosphorus and again up to the Atlantic Ocean through the Mediterranean Sea and the Gibraltar Strait.

On the East, ships can sail from the Bay of Bengal and the Indian Ocean to the countries of the Pacific Ocean through a number of Straits such as the Malacca Strait, Sunda Strait, Ombai Strait, etc, and the Timor Sea.

It also facilitates internal trade, commerce and communications through the rivers, notable among them being the Salween, Irawaddy, Ganges, Indus, Shatt-Al-Arab and Zambezi. Altogether these rivers drain an area of about 5,050,000 square miles and discharge into the Indian Ocean.[29]

The Persian Gulf area, where 62 per cent of the world's known oil reserves are located, has acquired immense global strategic interest. The entire seascape is involved in the quest for fuel oil. Most of this oil is being shipped across the Indian Ocean into the Red Sea towards the Suez or around the Cape of Good Hope to Europe or America or through the grand oceanic trunk road to the Strait of Malacca towards Japan, but also some is shipped to points on the Indian Ocean itself, to India, Australia and Singapore. And this ocean is also the thoroughfare of the transportation of other vital commodities (tin, rubber, foodstuffs, minerals, etc.) and so its geo-strategic significance cannot be denied or over-emphasized.[30]

It should also be remembered that individual countries are in the position of controlling the vital checkpoints leading to or from the Indian Ocean. A possible interference with vital traffic through these gateways could not be regarded as a local problem; it would develop into a question of regional or even global significance, should any of the naval powers try to place impediments to maritime transportation "anywhere" in the Indian Ocean, at the entry-exit points (such as the Cape) or elsewhere, all the area would immediately be involved. Nations of the two other oceans, geographically more decentralized, would not react in a similar manner. But if something like the Cuban missile crisis should arise, for instance, in the neighbourhood of Hormuz Strait or the Cape, an embargo on oil or other material commodities would set many countries aflame.[31]

Economic Importance of the Indian Ocean

The Seventies could be appropriately called **the decade of oceans**, when nations started looking towards the sea for their survival and prosperity. The Oceans, which cover Seven-tenth of the earth's surface (139,440,000 sq. miles), contain vast potential of food, hydro-carbons and mineral resources which are now man's greatest hopes for economic well being.[32]

The Oceans comprise 80 per cent of the world's fish stock, 90% of oil and natural gas reserves and a large number of other mineral resources. According to an estimate one square mile of sea bed contains 30,000 tones of manganese, 3,600 tones of aluminum, 2,300 tones of cadmium, 17,000 tones of iron, 400 tones of cobalt, 1,200 tones of nickel and 650 tones of copper.[33]

The Indian Ocean is rich in natural resources. Asia has the highest known offshore petroleum reserves, and the continental margins from India to Korea are reported to be among the most promising areas in the world. Even now the shallow waters of the Persian Gulf produce oil at the rate of more than 2.6 million barrels per day. Moreover, reservoirs beneath the gulf contain about 75 per cent of the worlds proven offshore reserves. Indonesia is the biggest oil producing and exporting region in Asia, and the recent successes, off the coast of Kalimantan and Sumatra, have spurred further activities on the vast, yet mainly unexplored, continental shelves. India, Sri Lanka and Bangladesh have also started searching for oil in the continental shelf area and their efforts have shown good promise. These oil explorations have gained great importance, especially after the so-called energy crisis of 1973. Besides oil, there are other minerals that can be exploited. The Red Sea has valuable copper deposits; other areas have not been explored so far for mineral resources other than oil. But as the capacity of littoral states to exploit their natural resources increases in the future, their resources in the continental shelf and beyond will be surveyed and possibly exploited. Marine products like fish and other seafood are another source of national wealth.[34]

The resources which we derive from the oceans can be broadly categorised as:

(1) Living, and

(2) Non-living.

Living Resources

In the category of living resources we may consider;

Capture fishery

Culture fishery/Mari-culture

Sea Weeds

Mangroves, and

Coral reefs.

The oceans have an average depth of 3,730 metres. The zone of maximum importance for mankind today, for the exploitation of natural living resources in the uppermost layer of 100 metres, is the zone where most of the photosynthetic production of organic matter occurs. It forms about 1.8 per cent of the world's oceans. From this zone more than 50 per cent of the world's fish catch is obtained at present. The regions occupying this zone are either fairly close to the coast or are in the very fertile areas of the coastal or offshore upwelling regions, called 'Oases" in the Sea. Since such areas constitute only 25 per cent of the total oceanic area, it can be assumed that 75 per cent of the ocean area may be termed obligotrophic with moderate to low production rates.

Capture Fishery

In India marine fish production consists largely of capture fisheries. At present India's marine fish production is of the order of 1.6 million tones, and India ranks sixth in the list of fish producing countries. India has also emerged as one of the foremost exporters of seafood in the world. The estimate for the potential fish yield of the Indian Ocean vary from about 7 million tones to 17 million tones.

Mariculture

Mariculture is not properly organized in India. It is largely based on traditional methods of trapping young prawns and fishes brought by tidal currents into enclosed areas where they are allowed to grow from three to nine months before harvesting. In India Sea farming is becoming popular now and it is expected to contribute to world aquaculture production to a great extent.

Seaweeds

Seaweed is one of the important living resources exploited by man for food, animal feed, fertilizers, chemicals and pharmaceutical products. The total marine algal yield of the world has been estimated at 172,000 tonnes per year. Of this India contributes only about two per cent of the total. The demand by industry for algal producing seaweeds (agrophytes) and alginproducing seaweed (alginophytes) is increasing very rapidly in India and abroad.

Mangrove Ecosystem

In India and in several other countries, mangrove ecosystems have been severely depleted during the last two decades. In the past, mangroves were treated as unwanted plants and were used largely as a source of timber and charcoal. It is only in recent years that they have been recognized as ecologically vital. Mangroves play a very important role in protecting the shoreline from major erosion. The ecosystem forms an ideal nursery for the juvenile forms of many economically important species such as mullet, sea trout and shrimps. A large per centage of detrital food, which supports a variety of young fishes and shrimps, is generated from mangroves.

Awareness of conservation issues and the need for the protection of the mangroves has been developing rapidly in most tropical and subtropical regions. By the year 2000, most of the shoreline of India was expected to be denuded of mangroves because of the pressure of population on land. Some mangrove forests will be protected as biosphere reserves. (We have two very famous mangrove forests in India - the Sunderbans and the Andaman and Nicobar Islands - both require conservation).

Coral Reefs

Coral reefs are among the most biologically productive, taxonomically diverse and aesthetically important living organisms. While their massive occurrence provides much needed protection from the waves to the coastline, their biological productivity yields a multitude of fauna and flora dependent on the coral reef ecosystem. They also provide opportunities for scuba diving, underwater photography, sport fishing and shell collecting, thus providing a vital stimulus to the tourist industry.

Due to population pressure, most of the coral reefs have become extremely vulnerable to industrial development and pollution along the coastline. Unless protection is offered to coral reefs, most of them will shrink in size in the future and ultimately die. Extensive protection is required in the form of coastal marine parks, to protect the fringing reefs along the main coastline of India. The reefs that will probably flourish are on the atolls of Lakshadweep and on some of the islands of the Andaman and Nicobar. The region was severely hit by the Tsunami on 26 December 2004. It may have destroyed these reefs. All efforts are being concentrated on saving man and material in the region and it is too soon to expect any solid information on the atoll's reefs of the islands.

Non-living Resources

Fresh water

Drugs from sea

Marine chemicals
Placer deposits
Offshore mining
Deep sea mining
Ocean Engineering

Fresh Water

Relative to population growth, the world supply of fresh water is dwindling rapidly every year and, therefore, measures are being undertaken to obtain drinking water from all possible sources. Several desalination technologies like solar stills, flash distillation technologies like electrodialysis and reverse osmosis are being employed to generate fresh water from seawater. In future this will play an important role for the supply of potable water to mankind.

Drugs from Sea

In India, the utilization of marine plants and animals as raw material for effective and safe drugs and pharmaceuticals is of recent origin. Of the 200 or more organisms that have been screened so far, many have given promising results. The most remarkable feature is the anti-fertility properties of several marine organisms. Research in this field and also on the culture of marine bacteria, fungi, yeast, and other organisms for the production of bioactive substances will advance considerably in the near future.

Marine Chemicals

Of the sixty elements present in seawater, only six are recovered economically. These are sodium and chlorine in the form of common salt, magnesium in the form of its compound, bromine, calcium and sulfur in the form of calcium sulfate (gypsum). Owing to its low concentration, the recovery of potassium directly from seawater is not considered economical. However, it is possible to recover potassium from bitterns (the mother liquor from slat extraction). Efforts are being made to recover many commercially useful elements from seawater, such as iodine, uranium and gold. So far, owing to the availability of cheaper extraction methods from land deposits, the technology of obtaining some of these valuable elements either from sea-water, sea brine or sea weed is not economical. Recently, a commercial process for the recovery of uranium from seawater has been reported and rapid development in this direction is expected.

Placer Deposits

These are mineral deposits found along the coastline and are seen on the exposed beeches. Mineral placers along the seashores, usually known as black sand, occur in many localities along the Indian coasts. These mainly contain ilmenite, rutile, zircon and monazite with varying proportions of magnetic and garnet value, and the importance of these is rapidly increasing and soon they will be exploited extensively.

Offshore Mining

The major minerals available from the sea are the minerals on the sea floor and in the seabed and minerals from seawater. From the ocean floor, coal, gold, diamond, tin, iron, phosphate, potash, sulfur and rare earth metals are being mined. Underwater tunneling, pumping and dredging are some of the expensive and hazardous techniques being used for off-shore mining.

By the turn of the century, the demand for almost all minerals will increase. Their production from land sources alone will be unable to meet the rising demand, and mankind will increasingly depend on the oceans for all these minerals.

Deep Sea Mining

In the past few years the development of technology to mine polymetallic nodules from a depth range of 4,000-5,000 meters and to extract the economically important metals from them has greatly advanced. In the 1960's nodules were recognized as the largest resource on the deep-sea bed. They exhibit varied physical and chemical properties and occur in different sizes (from 0.5 to 10 centimetres in diameter, though most of them are in the size range of 3-4 centimetres) and they are essentially porous. Generally, they have been described as dark, potato-shaped lumps. Their chemical composition also varies widely. In the near future they will become a very important source of minerals and the ocean's mineral worth will increase manifold.

Ocean Engineering

Engineering tasks associated with the ocean are many times more expensive than similar activities on land. Moreover the hazards of work are greater and the management of operations more demanding. The problems can be divided into five categories:

- Coastal zone management
- Control of coastal pollution
- Production of offshore oil and gas
- Control of coastal erosion, and
- Extraction of energy from the sea.

All these fields are rapidly gaining importance, and there is a great potential for developmental work to be carried out in these fields.

In India many premier organisations have been established to harness oceanic resources, such as:

- The Geological Survey of India
- The Oil and Natural Gas Commission
- Tata Institute of Fundamental Research
- India Meteorological Department
- The National Institute of Oceanography

- The Naval Hydrographic Office
- Central Fisheries Research Institute
- Engineers India Limited
- Port Development Authorities
- Beach Erosion Protection Boards, and
- Ocean Science and Technology Agency.[36]

Indian National Committee on Oceanic Research was initiated in 1960 to direct and coordinate the working of all these Institutes and Organizations.

To protect and safeguard her geopolitical, economic and security interests in the maritime environment through the Law of the Sea became one of India's prime objective. It is of special importance to India being a maritime nation having a vast coastline with a large continental shelf and economic zone full of living and non-living resources and a large number of islands in the Bay of Bengal and the Arabian Sea.[37] India has the added responsibility of safeguarding the maritime interests of its neighbouring landlocked countries i.e. Bhutan and Nepal.

In the present circumstances, resources of the Indian Ocean are mainly exploited by foreign maritime powers, and the countries of the region have to make a coordinated effort to save their maritime wealth and have control over their exploitation.

Efforts had started as early as the 1960's to bring as large an area as was possible of the high seas and the sea bed, under the authority of the United Nations, so that the marine powers which have a dominant voice in that organization, could continue to exploit their resources. The developing nations in the Indian Ocean area would not be able to hinder the marine powers from exploiting these resources because these powers would be working under the UN. An effort is being made to intimidate these small littoral states into accepting the new formula, and as a salve to their injured pride, it is suggested that the profits accruing to the UN out of these sea ventures would be used for the benefit of the developing countries. But from the very proposal it is evident that the motives of the marine powers are not entirely altruistic.[38]

The Maltese delegate Arvid Padro formally introduced the question in the General Assembly of the United Nations on 1st November 1967. He proposed that a new treaty should be drafted to prevent national appropriation of the seabed and ocean floor, to reserve those areas exclusively for peaceful purposes, to use the seabed assets primarily to benefit the developing countries and to restrict the limits of the continental shelf. He said that these goals could best be carried out by creating a new international agency on the lines of the World Bank to handle the problems of the oceans. The matter has been regularly debated in the UN ever since.

In 1970 a **"Declaration of Principles"** in the United Nations established that, "70 per cent of this planet's surface should be the **common heritage of mankind**. In an attempt to ensure that all people would reap equal benefit, it was resolved that a comprehensive treaty, a new sea law, as a complete package should be written."[39]

The General Assembly of the United Nations, by its resolution 3029 (XXVII) of 18 December 1972, decided to entrust the question of the codification of the new law of the sea to a world conference. Four conferences were held to codify the new law of the sea. After 9 years of deliberations, on 10 December 1982 at Montego Bay, Jamaica, the text was signed by the delegates of 117 States, and is known as UNCLOS III.[40]

The new law of the sea can be broadly divided into two main groups, one dealing with the sea-bed resources outside the limits of the State jurisdiction, and the other affecting the continental shelf, the territorial waters and the newly proposed economic zone.[41] As far as the law pertaining to the sea bed outside the limits of the state jurisdiction is concerned, two major trends are discernible. The developed countries, by and large, favour a free enterprise concept while the developing countries opt for a strong international authority to control this exploitation, and to prevent the multinationals from exploiting these resources to the detriment of the Third World countries.

India has taken a leading role in international forums on the enunciation of the laws of the sea, a vital subject to all littoral states, particularly, in the context of exploitation by the developed nations of under sea economic resources, untapped in the under developed regions. But, success in the Law of the Sea Conferences alone is not enough; it should be ensured that the international maritime law is revised by such conferences and agreements are strictly followed.[42]

The changing international concept on the freedom of the high seas has given rise to the formulation of an "Informal Composite Negotiating Act" produced by the United Nations Conferences on the Law of the Sea, which delineates the following outer limits:

(A) Territorial Sea-12 nautical miles from the base line.

(B) Contiguous Zone-24 nautical miles from the base line including the territorial sea.

(C) Exclusive Economic Zone-200 nautical miles from the base line of the territorial sea.

(D) The Continental Shelf - either 350 nautical miles from the base line of the territorial sea or 100 nautical miles from 2500 metres isobath.

The negotiating text having been produced largely by consensus and rarely by majority votes can be taken as the emerging trend in the regime of the high seas and is supported by India. The regime envisages that in the territorial sea, ships of all states shall enjoy innocent passage, not prejudicial to peace, good order or security of the coastal state.

For India the sea area that has come over under the Exclusive Economic Zone is well over two million square kilometres.

As for the continental shelf, so far as India is concerned, it stretches even beyond the Exclusive Economic Zone in certain areas.

To exploit India's maritime resources its National Institute of Oceanography, Goa, carried out explorations, and on the basis of the results India applied for a mine site in the Central Indian Ocean with the International Seabed Authority in January 1984 and ultimately after prolonged negotiations it was accepted and India was given the Pioneer investors status with only other three countries of the same status France, Japan and the USSR. India also became the first country of the world to have the registration of a mine site of 150000 square kilometres.[43]

India also has the privilege of being one of the fifteen countries, which are consultative parties under the Antarctica Treaty of 1959. As a result of having conducted substantial scientific activity, India gained entry into the group in 1983. Antarctica has considerable resources potential in the long term and is, therefore, one more area of maritime interest to India, in which there is much to be done.[44]

As India is one of the developed countries of the Indian Ocean region it has certain duties towards protecting the **environment** of the region and a great role to play in the region.

To solve the problems of disposal of nuclear wastes and other toxic industrial wastes some extra regional countries have begun looking towards the Indian Ocean Region. In fact the ship "Felicia" took toxic ash from the incinerators of Philadelphia and after failing to dump the same in many countries of Africa and Europe since August 1986, the vessel released its undesirable cargo off Bangladesh in the Bay of Bengal.[45]

Thus, it is not only the protection of shipping fleets and off shore installations from foreign interference but also protection and preservation of the marine environment and conservation of the living resources amongst other predicaments that require consideration on an economic dimension.

India: Changing Perceptions

For a long time the importance of the Indian Ocean for the security and commerce of India, was not adequately recognized. Most of the Indian historians in the past remained preoccupied with the Himalayas and the landmass beyond the Hidukush on the Northwest.

K.M. Panikkar was the first scholar who highlighted the significance of the Indian Ocean for the trade and security of India in his works published as early as in 1944-45[46]. Regretting the "unfortunate" tendency to overlook the sea in the discussion of India's defence problems he remarked, **"India never lost her independence till she lost the command of the sea in the first decade of the Sixteenth Century."**[47]

His views received support from another Indian author K.B. Vaidya who wrote, **"Even if we do not rule the waves of all the five oceans of the world, we at least must rule the waves of the Indian Ocean."**[48] Vaidya gave the call to convert the Indian Ocean into an **"Indian Lake"** which according to him meant that, **"India must have supreme and undisputed power over the waters of the Indian Ocean".**

India's approach to the problem of security in the Indian Ocean has been by and large in conformity with both the traditions of the anti-colonial struggle and the country's own enlightened self-interest. Having achieved her national freedom after a long struggle against foreign colonial rule, it should be naturally repugnant for India to think of dominating her neighbours in the name of safeguarding her security. India's approach has, therefore, got to be one of trying to realize security largely through promoting peaceful regional cooperation among the littoral and hinterland states and preventing the militarization of the Indian Ocean. The security of India and other littoral States of the Indian Ocean can hardly be ensured in a situation where the strategically located islands in the waters washing their shores are dotted with foreign military bases, and the naval task forces of outside great powers pose a threat to the national liberation movements practising gunboat diplomacy in a style reminiscent of the nineteenth century. In the present circumstances as emphasised by Panikkar and Vaidya, India just cannot afford to ignore its naval power as it has been doing in the recent past in the interests of regional security of the Indian Ocean Region. Hence, India has been insisting that the Indian Ocean should be left alone by the great powers as a **Sea of Peace**, a demand endorsed as early as at the Lusaka Conference of non-aligned nations in 1970, and at all subsequently held non-aligned Summits.[49]

After the end of cold war with the changing scenario of international politics, India's security perceptions have also changed. Now India is trying to modernise its navy in consonance with the changed and newly emerging security threats to its security. With the growing demands of its national security India has now been concentrating on making its navy the 'Blue water navy' after the last decade. This is a welcome change that has come a little late in India's security planning as other navies like those of China have started to make their presence felt in the region for quite sometime now. In the near future India will require a stronger navy not only to protect its own security and economic interests in the Indian Ocean but also to protect the interests of its immediate neighbours too.

References

1. Touissant, Auguste "History of the Indian Ocean", Chicago, pp. 5-6.

   (Vasco de Gama's arrival at Calicut is considered the dividing line between the Gaman and the Post-Gaman period of the history of the Indian Ocean.)

2. Pannikkar, K.M. "Asia and Western Dominance", Allen and Unwin, London, 1959, p. 22.
3. Bezboruah, Monoranjan "US Strategy in the Indian Ocean: The International Response", Prager, USA, 1977, p.2.
4. Pannikkar, K.M. *op. cit.*, p. 21.
5. Merit Students Encyclopedia Macmillan, Ed. Corp. New York, Vol. 14, p.7.
6. Mishra, R.N. "Indian Ocean and India's Security", Mittal Publications, Delhi, 1986, p.1.
7. Vali, F.A. "Politics of the Indian Ocean Region: The Balance of Power", The Free Press, New York, 1976, p.25.
8. Mishra, R.N. *op. cit.*, p.2.

   (According to Merit Students Encyclopedia, *op. cit.*, p. 13, it is Java trench off Java, 25, 344 feet, 7, 725 metres).
9. Buzan, Barry Survival Vol. 24, No. 1, Jan.-Feb. 1982, pp. 43-44.
10. *Ibid.*, p. 44.
11. Bezboruah, Monoranjan *op. cit.*, p.6
12. Miller, T.B. "The Military Strategic Balance" in Abbas Amirie (ed.). The Persian Gulf and The Indian Ocean in International Politics, Tehran, 1975, p. 80.
13. International Encyclopedia of Social Sciences, New York, 1968, Vol. 13, p. 378.
14. Palmer, Norman D. and Perkins, Howard C. "International Relations: The World Community in Transition" (New Delhi, 1985), first Indian edition. pp. 558-59.
15. Vali, F.A. *op. cit.*, pp. 24-43.
16. Yadav, R.S. "Regions in International Politics: A Study of the Indian Ocean", India Quarterly,.Vol. XLVII No. 1 & 2 Jan-June 1991, pp. 30-33.
17. Sharma, R.C. "The Indian Ocean and its Community: A Geographical Appraisal" in T.T. Poulose (ed.) Indian Ocean Power Rivalry, Young Asia, New Delhi 1974, p. 209.
18. Vali, F.A. *op. cit.*, p. 28.
19. Bhutto, Z.A. "The Myth of Independence" London, Oxford University Press, 1969, p. 26.
20. Vali, F.A. *op. cit.*, p. 31.
21. Bannerji, B.N. "Indian Ocean: A whirlpool of Unrest" Paribus, New Delhi, 1984, p. 9.

22. Vali, F.A. *op. cit.*, p. 32.
23. Pannikkar, K.M. "India and the Indian Ocean", London, 1957, pp. 18-19.
24. Cottrell, A.J. and Burrell, R.M. "The Indian Ocean: Its Political, Economic and Military Importance", Prager, New York, 1972, pp. 6-7.
25. Cole, G.D.H. "Imperial Military Geography", London, 1950, pp. 150-151.
26. *Ibid*, pp. 149-150.
27. Miller, T.B. "The Indian Ocean and Pacific Oceans: Some Strategic Considerations", London, 1969, p.3.
28. Vali, F.A. *op. cit.*, p. 37.
29. Bhattacharya, S.S. "Geo-Political Importance of the Indian Ocean", Strategic Analysis, Vol. XIV No. 7, Oct., 91, pp. 803-23.
30. Vali, F.A. *op. cit.*, p. 39.
31. Simpson, J. "The Indian Ocean Area: Zone of Disengagement or Balance of Power" in collected papers of the study conference on the Indian Ocean in International Politics, Southampton, England, 1973, p. 208.
32. Mishra, R.N. *op. cit.*, p. 38.
33. Vice Admiral M.K. Roy, "Changing Relations of the Sea to the State: The Need for a Ministry of Maritime Policy and Ocean Management", USI Journal, Vol. CX No. 459, Jan-March 1980.
34. Singh, K.R. "The Indian Ocean: Big Power Presence and Local Response", Manohar, New Delhi, 1977, pp. 263-264.
35. Qasim, S. Zahoor "The Oceans: The Future Hope of Mankind", pp. 29-44. In Satish Chandra, B. Arunachalam and V. Suryanarayan (ed.) "The Indian Ocean and its Islands: Strategic, Scientific and Historical Perspectives", Sage, New Delhi, 1993.
36. Kohli, S.N. "Sea Power and the Indian Ocean: With Special Reference to India". Tata McGraw Hill, New Delhi, 1978, pp. 64-65.
37. Mishra, R.N. *op. cit.*, p. 92.
38. Singh, K.R. *op. cit.*, pp. 264-265.
39. Forbes, Vivian L. "Implementation and Ratification of UNCLOS", Indian Ocean Review Australia, December 1991, Vol. 4, No. 4.
40. *Ibid*.
41. Singh, K.R. *op. cit.*, p. 266.

42. Rear Admiral K. Sridharan, A Maritime History of India, (New Delhi, 1982), Publication Division, Ministry of Information and Broadcasting, Govt. of India, pp. 348-350.
43. Qasim, Zahoor. *op. cit.*, pp. 39-40.
44. *Ibid*., p. 67.
45. Capt. H. Dharamrajan, "India's Role in the context of Indian Ocean Security", USI Journal, Jan-March 1990, Vol. C, No. 499, pp. 186-187.
46. Pannikkar, K.M. "The Strategic Problems of the Indian Ocean", Allahabad, 1944.
47. Pannikkar, K.M. "India and the Indian Ocean," *op. cit.*, p. 14.
48. Vaidya, K.B. "The Naval Defence of India" Bombay. 1947, p. 91.
49. Kaushik, D. "The Indian Ocean: A Strategic Dimension", Vikas, 1985, Delhi, pp. 86-87.

2

Conceptualizing Peace

Peace as a concept is like motherhood, noble, eminently desirable and essential for the continuation of mankind.[1] A 'Zone of Peace' has the additional ingredient of being sufficiently unprecise and all-embracing to make it even more suitable as an issue to support, yet vague enough to be capable of varied interpretations to suit one's own perception. Peace is moreover so positively 'loaded' that no individual or country can come out against a plan or aim thus labelled without immediately incurring moral opprobrium[2]. This ensures that it receives wide acceptance as an issue in the international agenda but its concretisation as a plan of action remains elusive.

More than three decades have passed since the then Prime Minister of Sri Lanka Mrs. Sirimao Bandarnaike formally raised the question of Peace Zone in the Indian Ocean. In her speech on 8 Oct. 1964 at the second non-aligned nations conference at Cairo, she forcefully argued that the concept of a **Nuclear Peace Zone** should be applied to the oceans also, especially to the oceans like the Indian ocean and the South Atlantic which had remained free from nuclear weapons till then. These suggestions were subsequently incorporated in the declaration of the Cairo Conference, which is also known as the *"Programme for Peace and International Cooperation"*.[3] Over the years support to the proposal, which was formally passed by the United Nations General Assembly in December 1971, has increased manifold.

Here a few questions may be asked:

1. How did the concept of peace zone originate?

2. What is the meaning of the concept of a Zone of Peace?
3. What preconditions should be fulfilled to establish a Zone of Peace?
4. What are the aims and objectives behind the demand for a Zone of Peace?
5. What are the alternatives available if a Peace Zone cannot be established? and,
6. What are the principles of Peace?

Origin of The Concept

The origin of the concept of the Indian Ocean as a Zone of Peace can be traced to various measures adopted and under consideration in pursuit of disarmament in the early 1960's.[4]

The Antarctica Treaty of 1959 had prohibited the establishment of military bases and fortifications and carrying out of military manoeuvre and nuclear explosions in the Antarctic.

The then Soviet Union had submitted proposals to the United Nations in 1959 for the creation of a nuclear-free Zone in Central Europe.[5]

The Partial Test Ban Treaty of 1963 prohibited nuclear weapon test explosions in the atmosphere, outer space and underwater.

In 1963, the General Assembly, through its resolution No. 1911 (XVIII), approved the denuclearization of Latin America.[6]

Outer Space Treaty of 1967 prohibited placing into the orbit nuclear weapons or weapons of mass destruction.[7]

Tlateloco Treaty of 1967 sought to prohibit the testing, use, manufacture, production or acquisition of any nuclear weapons by the Latin American countries.[8]

The Non-Proliferation Treaty of 1968 prohibited the transfer of nuclear weapons and material by nuclear weapon states to non-nuclear weapon states and prohibited the latter from acquiring nuclear weapon capability, while not restricting in any way the vertical proliferation of states that already had nuclear weapons.

The Seabed Treaty of 1971 prohibited the emplacement of nuclear weapons installations and facilities on the seabed beyond the outer limit of 12 nautical miles.

The Biological Weapons Convention of 1972 prohibited the development, production, stockpiling or requisition of biological agents.[9]

The aims of highlighting all these developments is to show that the advocates of Indian Ocean Peace Zone had sound precedents to go by and the concept as such is not just visionary and therefore is worthy of serious consideration. It shows that prevailing feelings in the world, at that time, as far as signing peace treaties was concerned, was very positive and optimistic.

Meaning

The concept of Peace as it is generally understood means pacification or appeasement, originating from a Latin word Pax Pacis. It emphasizes a state of quiet or freedom from disturbance, conflict or war.[10] There are two divergent shades of the concept one signifying a condition referring to the absence of turmoil, tension, conflict and war; the other refers to **peace** achieved by good management, orderly resolution of conflict and the establishment of harmony and tranquility through understanding and negotiations.

A Zone of Peace can be defined as a geographical area from where the danger of war is eliminated by resolving tensions.[11] The defusion of tension causing danger of war involves two fundamental projections: one, to promote cordial relations among the regional nations, irrespective of their might and influence on corporate basis as equal partners, and two, to make it necessary for the outside military presence to stage an exit from the region. The increasing interdependence among nations and regions does not allow the carving out of any particular area, especially if it is of great geo-strategic importance, as such has a bearing on the politico-military developments of the world. Similarly, it would be quite difficult to resolve completely the mutual rivalries and restore confidence in the regional countries. There is, therefore, a great need in some regions of the world, which are susceptible to tensions in the near future, such as the Indian Ocean, to establish a Zone of Peace:[12]

> For the establishment of peace it is necessary to reverse the process of war. The stages that emerge are the transition from stable war to unstable war, from unstable war to unstable peace, and from unstable peace to stable peace by deliberate decision, broad and general and do not refer to the prerequisites of establishing a stable peace.[14]

The concept of the Indian Ocean as a Zone of Peace conforms to the present international development. It is an extension of the spirit of détente to this region. It was first used as a slogan to keep the Cold War off this region and now, it is against the policy of threats, intimidations, pressures and blackmail in the changed circumstances.

A Zone of Peace means in the first place the dismantling of all the existing military blocs in the Indian Ocean Region.

It implies that no foreign power ever threatens the independence, sovereignty, security and territorial integrity of the littoral and hinterland States.

It also implies that the Indian Ocean must not be used for furthering the neo-colonialist's designs, and, above all,

The Indian Ocean must not be used for the global policy of war and aggression. It is aimed at abrogation of military pacts.[13]

The concept of Peace Zone has five major aspects:

First, the Resolution of a nuclear-free Zone, which figured in the 1970 Lusaka Conference. It was confirmed by the United Nation's General Assembly in 1971, The UN assembly urged the United States, the then Soviet Union, Britain and France, which had the capability of deploying nuclear weapons in the area to renounce the nuclear-build-up. It also enjoined upon the regional countries to give an undertaking that they would neither allow external powers to build up nuclear bases, in their territories nor would they develop nuclear war potential themselves.

Secondly, the resolution aimed at halting the further escalation and expansion of their (Great powers) military presence in the Indian Ocean and eliminating all bases, military installations and logistical supply facilities, the disposition of nuclear weapons and weapons of mass destruction, and any other manifestation of great power military presence in the area, conceived in the context of great power rivalry. It was incorporated at the instance of Sri Lanka.[15]

Thirdly, to achieve the elimination of great power rivalries and competition from the Indian Ocean Region, it necessitated, besides the measures for arms control and disarmament, the adoption of political measures to promote peace, security and solidarity in the region.

Fourthly, the Resolution also stressed the need for settling the regional disputes through peaceful means and mutual negotiations without any external interference. It also called upon the regional powers to accept the obligation of controlling arms and affecting disarmament along with controlling and resolving intra-regional disputes.[16]

Lastly, the resolution envisaged the elimination of colonialism and racism from the Oceanic Islands and the mainland of Afro-Asia. The Resolution in the end called upon all states to "consider and respect the Indian Ocean as a Zone of Peace from which great power rivalries and competitions," whether army, navy or airforce, are excluded. The area should be free of nuclear weapons.[17] Realising that the major responsibility fell on the littoral states in the implementation of the Resolution, Mrs. Bandaranaike, the then Prime Minister of Sri Lanka, urged that "all countries bordering the Indian Ocean should join us not only in giving effect to this proposal but also in keeping the Indian Ocean as an area of peace.[18]

Pre-conditions

The resolution of the United Nations General Assembly highlights certain premises and conditions, which are basic to its concept of a Zone of Peace in the Indian Ocean. These are:

- The determination of the peoples of the littoral and hinterland states of the Indian Ocean to preserve their independence, sovereignty and territorial integrity.
- Rejection of the use of the Indian Ocean by warships and military air crafts for any threat or use of force against the sovereignty, territorial integrity and independence of any littoral or hinterland state of the Indian Ocean.
- Elimination from the Indian Ocean of all bases, military installations, logistical supply facilities, disposition of nuclear weapons and weapons of mass destruction and extension of the arms race by the great powers, halting the further escalation and expansion of great power military presence in the Indian Ocean, in the context of great power rivalry and competition, and pursuit of the objectives of establishing a system of universal collective security without military alliances, through regional forums of cooperation.[19]

In the context of the Peace Zone in the Indian Ocean it has been suggested that not only measures of arms control and disarmament, but also political measures to promote peace and security in the region, be strengthened.[20]

The concept 'Zone of Peace' thus seeks to ensure that neither would the non-littoral states, in future, have permanent naval forces stationed in the Indian Ocean nor would they seek military bases in the region, as militarisation of the Indian Ocean is a matter of grave concern to all the countries of the region.

The adoption of the policy of non-alignment by a majority of the regional nations is a step towards the fulfillment of their desire to transform the Indian Ocean into a Zone of Peace as a "necessary condition for maintaining and preserving their political independence and sovereignty.[21] The creation of a Peace Zone in the Indian Ocean was also expected to be a positive step towards the reduction of tensions in the region and as such to contribute to the strength of international peace and solidarity.

Aims and Objectives

The struggle for a Zone of Peace in the Indian Ocean must be based on concrete objectives and tasks i.e.,

- Liquidation of all military bases of foreign powers and unconditional withdrawal therefrom of their navy, army and airforce units.
- Prohibiting the use of the Ocean to submarines, aircraft carriers or other naval vessels armed with nuclear bombs or missiles.
- Agreement between the states of the Indian Ocean region not to manufacture or stockpile nuclear weapons on their territories and to restrict their nuclear capabilities to peaceful uses only.
- Promotion by mutual cooperation of the countries concerned of a system of regional collective security on the basis of equality, thereby paving the way for peaceful settlement of outstanding military and political conflicts in the region, stronger economic cooperation in the interests of independent and self-reliant development and stable peace. For the realization of these aims not only the governments, but the peoples of the Indian Ocean Region must exercise, in a more vigorous and coordinated manner, their utmost initiatives, vigilance and mobilization.[22]

Here it may be asked how the concept of Peace Zone relates to the foreign policy objectives of the littoral and hinterland States?

Arms control proposals of any kind by any state fulfil foreign policy objectives of three kinds:

- Strategic,
- Political-psychological, and
- Diplomatic.

The strategic objective underlying the arms control proposals that a State puts forward is the attempt to improve its military position relative to that of its rivals. It would improve the military position of the littoral and hinterland states relative to that of the external powers by removing the nuclear weapons, other military presence and spheres of influence of the latter, while leaving the former free to establish nuclear forces, increased armed forces and spheres of influence of their own. Hopes for such an eventuality provide an important part of the impetus behind the "Zone of Peace" proposal particularly for the larger states of the region such as India.[23]

The political psychological objective that underlies the arms control proposals is the attempt through propaganda directed at third parties to bring pressure to bear on political opponents. The canvassing of the "Zone of Peace" proposal, whether or not it has any prospect of being realised, provides the littoral States with the opportunity to mobilize opposition to the activities of the external power to which, in varying degrees, they are opposed - the Soviet and United States naval patrols in the area, maintenance by the United States, Britain and France of bases and other installations, and pursuit by the Soviet Union of such bases or off shore facilities, British and French maintenance of colonial possessions and the continuing links between the western powers and the white supremacist state of Southern Africa.

The diplomatic objective underlying the arms control proposals is the attempt to identify common interests with other states in the field of military policy and to devise means whereby these common interests may be advanced. It is only when the third objective predominates over the first and the second in the policies of the states affected by an arms control proposal that there is any prospect that negotiation will get underway and that an agreement will be reached.

The littoral and hinterland states of the Indian Ocean Region have not yet demonstrated that they can translate a vague perception of common interests vis-a-vis the great powers into precise proposals. There are profound differences of approach.

On the question of a nuclear free zone there is a division between India, which at first wanted to preserve the option of acquiring nuclear weapons, (and now has exercised its option) and those which contend that restrictions should be imposed on zonal powers also.

On the issue of the military presence of the Great Powers there is a potential division between those regional states such as India, Iran and Indonesia - which in the absence of Great Power military influence would be dominant in their immediate neighbourhoods, and those smaller states which would prefer to see some military influence of the Great powers remain, to provide a check to that dominance; the concerns of Sri Lanka and Pakistan about India, of Iraq about Iran and of Singapore about India - are cases in point.

As regards the banishment from the area of Great Power alliances, this can be hardly regarded in the same light by Iran, Pakistan and Australia, which are allies of the United States, nor by India, Iraq and Bangladesh, which were internal allies of the Soviet Union, as it can by states whose stance is "generally non-aligned".

If the Indian Ocean were to become a nuclear-free zone this might enhance the objective of international security in two ways. If the Zone was defined in such a way as to include the territory of the littoral states, it would be an instrument for combating the proliferation of nuclear weapons. Moreover, whether or not it included the littoral states territory, the exclusion of nuclear weapons from the sea, the air above it and the seabed, would remove the danger that a nuclear war might arise out of an incident involving nuclear weapons in that area.

The limitation, reduction or elimination of the former Soviet Union, American, British and French military presence might be expected to lessen the danger that these powers will threaten the security of local states, and also to reduce the prospects of their coming into conflict with each other.

The elimination of Great power rivalries and tensions from the area might remove a source of conflict among regional states caught up in them.

There are five kinds of proposals that have advanced the project of a Zone of Peace in the Indian Ocean.[24]

First, there are proposals to render the Indian Ocean a nuclear-free zone.

Second, there are proposals to eliminate, reduce, restrict or halt the further expansion of the military presence of the Great Powers in the area.

Third, there are proposals, which call for the elimination of Great Power rivalries and competition from the area, as distinct from the removal of bases conceived in the context of such rivalries and competition.

Fourth, there are proposals, which concern the settling of disputes or the acceptance of arms control restrictions among the littoral and hinterland states themselves.

Finally, there are proposals, which assert a connection between the prospects of peace in the Indian Ocean and one or other political objective of the littoral and hinterland states.

Since the concept of Peace Zone was taken up, some scholars and statesman, optimistic about the establishment of the concept, have suggested hypothetically the following **conditions and tendencies which tend to create a hope for the realization of a Peace Zone in the Indian Ocean.**[25]

First, the aspiration of the regional states to strengthen their sovereignty and independence against the hegemonic drives and great power rivalries lends considerable support to the idea of a Peace Zone as it is expected "to eliminate, within the specified limits, all those manifestations which endanger the achievement of regional aspirations."[26]

Second, the growing sense of dissatisfaction with the concept of balance of power as the basis of international peace and security correspondingly increases the awareness amongst the regional powers of the necessity of accepting the Indian Ocean as a Zone of Peace.

Third, to achieve universal peace, end of arms race and elimination of fear of a nuclear war, it would be necessary to move forward to that end by stages, i.e. by first carving out Zones of Peace, as universal peace still appears to be a distant hope. The establishment of Peace Zones therefore seeks spatially limited applications wherever a people or group of people wishes to ensure conditions of security.

Fourth, the dis-inclination of the regional States to accept the political alternatives of liberal democracy and communism as offered by the two great powers, create a hope of the success of the Peace Zone idea as the non-alignment tends to coalesce the ideologies and avoid bipolarity in international politics.

Fifth, the general desire of mankind to contribute positively towards détente, international security and peace also necessitates outside powers' disengagement and withdrawal from as many areas or regions of the world as possible from the game of power struggle.

Sixth, regional and international cooperation is likely to occur when states face problems that are insoluble domestically and cost unbearably[27]. This is particularly true of the Afro-Asian region.

Seventh, the non-aligned countries in principle are more or less Peace Zones because their territories, air space and territorial waters are not available for the purpose of the contening powers and ideologies. This can also serve as launching pads for the establishment of Peace Zones.

Eight, The concept of Peace Zone is expected to provide the transitional minimum conditions for development of an Indian Ocean Community in which problems of security will be dealt with by orderly and institutional means for promoting peaceful changes,[28] and

Last, in view of the past developments in South Asia, Southeast Asia, the Middle East and Africa, specially Iran and Afghanistan and also everywhere else, where nuclear arms are present, the possibility of naval war cannot be ruled out completely. There is an acute awareness among the regional nations that such a war, automatically involving the big powers, would be highly detrimental to their socio-economic development and sovereignty.

Lest such an analysis should appear simple and misleading, it may be mentioned that hope is juxtaposed with despair. It should not be misconstrued that the Peace Zone in the Indian Ocean is not fraught with many complexities inherent in the present situation. Moreover the delay in the implementation of the resolution tends to heighten skepticism in certain diplomatic circles that the concept is both impractical and unworkable. The concept of Peace Zone in the Indian Ocean no longer seems viable under the existing international circumstances.[29]

Problems and Obstructions

In the implementation of the concept there are some problems:

First, having its origin in the basic tenets of nonalignment the concept of Peace Zone has been inextricably linked with the developments in the region.

Second, the concept as is generally understood relates to pacification or appeasement. The absence of the clash of interests of the community of nations as an essential condition of peace is highly unpragmatic.

Third, the most difficult problem is created by the involvement of the external powers in the regional affairs. To pursue them in favour of the elimination of competition and mutual rivalries in the Indian Ocean region is in itself a Herculean task.

Fourth, as the concept of Peace Zone in the Indian Ocean has wide ramifications, it would be unfair to presume that it can be achieved by exterminating the external powers because, even if the external powers agree to withdraw from the region, the regional problems and differences would continue to pose insurmountable challenges to the peace in the region. Some of the smaller and weaker states of the Indian Ocean region suspect the bigger and stronger states of the area in the context of their own security and development. The irony of the situation, therefore, is that the regional powers are supporting the concept of Peace Zone on the one hand and are seriously concentrating on their military / naval build-up on the other which is bound to encourage a scramble for dominance within the region.

Fifth, despite the geographic homogeneity of the region the relationship among the states of the Indian Ocean presents a kaleidoscopic structure. In view of this, the future of regional cooperation would continue to be bilateral or sub-regional which in a situation of conflict or crisis is bound to be influenced by the external military presence in the region.

Sixth, the external powers make the issues further complicated by their criticism that the purpose of the concept amounts to a gross transgression of the freedom of the seas and the prevailing customary and conventional international laws of the Sea.

Seventh, some experts feel that the UN treatment of the Peace Zone concept is marked by "Over-simplification, misrepresentation, euphemism and the attitude of can't."[30] Also it lacks clarity regarding the curbing of oceanic movements.

Eight, the problem has been further complicated by the reluctance of the big powers and other maritime users of the Indian Ocean in favour of the resolution which amounts to putting the cart before the horse and making it ineffective in its implementation and have encouraged some of the smaller states to adopt a hostile or apathetic attitude towards the concept while convincing the others to consider it too ambitious and premature.[31]

Ninth, with the end of the cold war and other developments in South Asia and Southeast Asia naval rivalry between the big and even non-traditional naval powers like China and India has increased instead of declining. Non-traditional threats to the maritime security of nations have increased manifold thus resulting in larger naval deployment making the establishment of peace in the Indian Ocean even more difficult.

Last but not the least high hope had generated with the establishment of IOR-ARC. The association was expected to bring the states of the Indian Ocean closer and promote cooperation among them. Since its establishment in 1997 it has not been much successful and has not made its presence felt in international forums. This has caused serious doubts as to the success of any association for regional cooperation in the region.

Practically, the concept has two dimensions; one that of the regional states whose immediate concern is security and economic survival. Their vision of world peace does not transcend the regional barriers because they are not developed enough to have a global view of the problem. While the other dimension is that the regional peace is a step towards global peace. In this case, the Peace Zone concept becomes subservient to the latter. Therefore, the concept of a Peace Zone in the Indian Ocean is believed to be inseparable from the global peace and unrealizable till the global peace is established.

The package of the Peace Zone in the Indian Ocean can be sub-divided into four more or less independent variables in the sense that the fulfillment of one is not necessarily dependent upon that of the other. In other words if efforts are made to work out a solution of these variables even independently, the total efforts would amount to achieving the Peace Zone in the Indian Ocean in easy stages if necessary. These four variables are:

First, great power rivalry in the context of the Cold War, and even after the end of cold war especially regarding the deployment of the strategic nuclear weapons systems.

Second, the question of denuclearization, especially when perceived from the point of view of the nuclear weapons powers and the non-nuclear weapons powers. Such a difference in perception is also reflected in the global vs. regional approach to the question of denuclearization.

Third, the need to evolve a non-aligned security doctrine which can present an alternative to the existing doctrine based upon the use of force and the inevitability of conflict i.e. based upon the concept of man that is essentially Hobbesian in nature, and

Last, the non-aligned states, through not a part of the bloc systems, are part of the present global system. To be effective, especially while bargaining with the Great Powers, these states, singly or collectively, must demonstrate their capability to fulfil their obligations towards the international community whether they be in the context of the basic issues of peace and security or the more mundane question of guaranteeing the freedom of navigation in major sea lanes. Unless they are able to demonstrate the capability, others would not only ignore them but also feel free to take some actions as they might deem appropriate to safeguard their own national interests. Thus, these states are duty-bound to create conditions whereby they can individually or collectively contribute effectively to the maintenance of international order, at least in their region.[32]

Alternative proposal and confidence-building measures

If the Peace Zone in the Indian Ocean means freedom of navigation, of trade and commerce, and of cultural interaction, then exceptions apart, the Indian Ocean was a Peace Zone till the advent of European maritime colonialism in the fifteenth century. All the three main components of the Peace Zone concept were destroyed by the Europeans who sought to establish their monopolies over them.[33]

The entire move to have a Zone of Peace in the Indian Ocean arose on account of the activities of outside powers, particularly the Super Powers. **What means and method then are available to the advocates of the Peace Zone proposal to persuade or compel the outside Powers to change their present attitude?**

K.P. Mishra suggests some theoretical levels, i.e.:

- If all the Afro-Asian countries join hands and boycott outside powers, in certain respects, it may create some real difficulties for the latter set of countries.
- If the supply of some essential raw material e.g. oil, is stopped, the outside powers are likely to face problems not easily surmountable.
- It is also suggested that a step easier and more effective than all this is a threat by the Indian Ocean littoral countries to withdraw from the Non-Proliferation Treaty (NPT), the Asian African membership of which the super powers consider very important. Continued adherence to the NPT by Afro-Asian countries should be made contingent on the great powers acceptance of the Peace Zone proposal.

Here two points need to be explored. **First**, if there is a collective action by the countries of Asia and Africa, other powers are bound to retaliate. **Second**, a concerted effort on the part of the Asian and African Countries presupposes their deep commitment to the Peace Zone idea and firm determination to swim or sink together.

To expect a really united action is to take an over-optimistic view of the situation and to minimize the difference in outlook among the Afro-Asian countries themselves.

In order to establish a Peace Zone regime, a series of multilateral agreements and treaties will have to be concluded on sensitive and controversial issues, to make progress step by step.

Though all the permanent members of the Security Council excepting China and all outside maritime users of the Indian

Ocean excepting Japan refused to cooperate with the countries of the area on the question of the Peace Zone for the Indian Ocean, and the demand had originated due to the western presence in the area, still the US and the Soviet Union also suggested a few alternative proposals to the concept of the Zone of Peace.

- A Soviet Government memorandum submitted to the United Nations in December 1964 entitled "Measures for further Easing of International Tension and Restructuring the Arms Race" devoted a section to the question of establishing nuclear free zones and proposed the Indian Ocean as one such zone. This proposal did not evoke any notable response from other nations, and it seems that in subsequent years the Soviet efforts also became somewhat dormant, for a variety of reasons. The Soviet Union took two initiatives in the year 1971. According to a US Government Spokesman in the spring of 1971 "*mutual naval restraint*" was informally suggested by the Soviets.[35] In June the same year Moscow had again proposed to Washington that the limitation of naval forces be discussed. Apart from this, however, no specifics and details were reported.
- Several Americans, including members of Congress, academics and even public officials, have made suggestions, which in effect constitute alternatives to the peace Zone proposals.
- Elliot Richardson, when he was under Secretary of the State urged that the USA should acknowledge and develop, "Spheres of restraint" particularly in areas such as the Indian Ocean, where competition had not yet become acute.[36]

Such statements facilitate the task of exploring solutions for the problems:

- Howard Wriggins of the South-East Asia Institute, Columbia University, (New York) suggested that "the best way to avoid a new arms race in the Indian Ocean would seem to negotiate a formal neutralization agreement among the US, the Soviet Union, Britain, France and the littoral States." (If possible, the Peoples Republic of China could also be included...) If a full neutralization of the Indian Ocean should prove unrealizable, a less ambitious agreement might at least limit the numbers and types of naval vessels each Super Power could introduce here at any given time.[37]

- William Brands of the US Council on Foreign Relations (New York) pleaded for the establishment of a *'Low level presence'* through some of the arms control measures between the United States and the Soviet Union.[38]
- Kennedy-Pell resolution of 1974.[39] While the Peace Zone proposal proposes to eliminate all activity by outside powers in the region that have the potential for generating tensions, the proposals emanating from the Untied States seek to limit or control the Super Power presence and rivalry in the area.

All this lip service to the concept apart, nothing much has been achieved in the direction of implementing the concept of a Peace Zone in the Indian Ocean. The world strategic environment has changed since the acceptance of the concept, and in the changed circumstances confidence-building measures can be the only alternative towards implementation of the concept of Zone of Peace in the Indian Ocean.

There is no alternative to faith in Peace, ultimate elimination of all weapons of mass destruction, general and complete disarmament and cooperative international order. So, it is necessary to start with pragmatic and easily achievable **confidence-building measures** in order to build up the momentum for relatively more complex measures at a later date. Some of these confidence-building measures suggested by K. Subrahmanyam are:[40]

First, convening of the Indian Ocean Peace Zone Conference without elaborate preconditions,

Second, to restore the humanitarian rights of the displaced island people of Diego Garcia,

Third, the acceptance and implementation of a zero-zero option in respect of deployment of extra-regional navies in the Indian Ocean, especially of the two foremost military powers.

Fourth, the countries of the Indian Ocean littoral and possibly including the erstwhile Soviet Union and China should conclude a convention not to use their nuclear capabilities against each other and declare that the use and the threat of use of nuclear weapons (except in retaliation) will be deemed as outlawed; this will be a valuable contribution for de-proliferation efforts,

Fifth, the idea of an international conference of energy exporters and importers (particularly of oil) should be revived and the security of energy source as well as the pattern of energy use with reference to the adverse impact of Green house effect should be considered.

Sixth, the Indian Ocean Peace Zone Conference should be converted into a continuing conference which could discuss the twenty substantive issues and principles formulated by the Indian Ocean Ad hoc Committee Working Group and arrive at a settlement of various issues in stages over a period of time.

Principles for Peace

Peace is not merely the absence of war or active hostility. To have real meaning and relevance, it must have wide connotations. Peace must aim at creating a dynamic environment that promotes harmony and equity in international relations. For such kind of positive peace there are a few principles which have to be realised in order to implement the concept of Zone of Peace in the Indian Ocean. These principles are:

First, the removal of external powers from the region, even if their interest in the area may be legitimate. The presence of outside elements and influences to protect and safeguard these interests cannot be justified. The concept of external presence includes not only the armed forces of these nations but also other means of exerting coercive pressures. Their removal is extremely difficult to achieve, but with regional consumers, progress can be made, albeit slowly. The modalities for this would need to be carefully evolved but, with greater awareness of the danger of external presence and by strengthening regional organisations, it should be possible to provide a better capability to withstand external coercion.

Second, development of regional initiatives to resolve conflicts. The UN should have been able to play a major role in ensuring peace in the world, but it has otherwise been occupied with security problems e.g. the Iran-Iraq war, Kampuchea and Afghanistan. The UN response on these has been ineffective, absent and delayed. In the current Indian Ocean environment, regional initiatives are likely to have better prospects in settling regional disputes. Each region will need to plan out its respective framework for such tasks.

Third, adoption of democratic methods in solving problems. Essentially, problems are created by people and without effective people's participation solutions cannot hold. Therefore, democratic frameworks are important. It is neither feasible nor desirable to lay down a single democratic path that all must follow. Each country must adopt the pattern that best suits the genius of its own people, but it needs to be based on genuine people's participation and democratic institutions. At the same time, minority interests must not be trampled upon by brute majority opinion.

Fourth, regional peacekeeping, which is a complex issue. The term was formalised by the UN in 1965, but it has not been possible for the world body to define it. An accepted definition adopted by the International Peace Academy is, the prevention, containment, moderation and termination of hostilities between or within states through the medium of third party intervention, organised and directed internationally, using multinational, military, police and civilian personnel to restore and maintain peace. By its very nature, peacekeeping is non-coercive and in many cases non-mandatory and depends on the initiatives and consent of the parties to the conflict to achieve consensus and later cooperation. In this difficult role careful planning and preparation is needed. Knowledge of the local environment and regional sensitivities is important. Hence regional actors best play the role preferably under the guidance of a regional organisation.[41]

The Concept of Zone of Peace has certain serious and immediate implications e.g.:

As the concept is discussed in the perspective of disarmament and world peace,[42] it is generally misunderstood as a collective security plan of a group of nations of the region which is misconstrued by some nations as the emergence of a regional power block, vis-a-vis, external power blocks. Howard Wriggins feels that the imaginative participation in the coalition building process now promoted by the littoral states may be more influential, in fact, in all but worst contingencies, than a costly naval presence.[43] This is probably the reason why, "there has been so far no agreement whatsoever, nor are there any signs of one in the immediate future"[44] regarding conversion of the idea into a reality.

- One of the significant pre-conditions is the adoption of the principle of denuclearization with an advanced aim of renouncing nuclear weapons. To some nations like India, this precondition is not acceptable as it allows the external powers to develop their nuclear weapons and prohibit the regional powers to do so. The problem of disarmament and nuclear weapons pertains to all the countries of the world. Therefore, in their opinion it cannot be settled regionally. India's refusal to sign the non-proliferation treaty has encouraged Pakistan to acquire the "Islamic Bomb". The problem can become still more complicated in view of the regional states which abstain from going nuclear.[45]

- The proposition involving renunciation by the regional nations of mutual threats or use of force against each other does not appear to be feasible in view of the recent political developments. Although a majority of the littoral states agree to the proposal in principle yet on account of their varied problems, divergent perspectives and priorities, a different continental outlook urging upon them to develop individual naval ambitions further complicates the situation beyond control in relation to the idea of a Peace Zone. The irony of situation is that the regional nations are supporting the concept of Peace Zone, on the one hand, and are concentrating on their own naval build-up, on the other, which is destined to develop into a scramble for dominance within the region.

- Support to the idea of Peace Zone in the Indian Ocean appears to be gradually fading out on account of the militarist attitude in the region and refusal to solve mutual problems through negotiations.[46]

- Militarization of the Atlantic and The Pacific Ocean and the Mediterranean Sea does not permit this Ocean, vital from the geo-strategic and economic angles, to continue as an area without competitions. The great powers have been continuously increasing their military presence in accordance with their national requirements.

- Emergence of mutual fear and suspicion and apprehension of mutual attack is the legacy of the world war II; despite creation of the United Nations, use of force has emerged as a national phenomenon to settle international disputes and very little attention has been paid to the UN decisions and resolutions.

- It is quite improbable to achieve international security through prohibition of nuclear proliferation in a particular area, especially when such a prohibition has a considerable bearing on relations between the countries in the Zone of Peace and the countries outside it as, for example, relationship between India and China.[47]

The problem arising out of the implementation of the concept has worldwide dimensions. Therefore, there is a need to clearly define the concept, explain the *modus vivendi* to implement it and persuade both the regional and the external powers to see utility of the idea in terms of establishing peace in the world.

References

1. Bannerji, D. "Indian Ocean Zone of Peace: Need for a New Approach", Strategic Analysis, vol. XV, No. 8, Nov. 1992, p. 173.
2. Braun, D. "The Indian Ocean Region of Conflict or Peace Zone?" Oxford University Press, Delhi, 1983, p. 172.
3. Singh, K. Rajendra "Politics of the Indian Ocean", Thomson, New Delhi, 1974, p. 181.
4. Harrison, Selig & Subrahamanyam, K. "Super Power Rivalry in the Indian Ocean, Indian and American Perspectives" Oxford University Press, New Delhi, 1989, p. 224.
5. Sipri Year Book 1968/69 World Armaments and Disarmament, Stockholm Int. Peace Research Institute, pp. 298-99.
6. *Ibid.*, pp. 308-309.
7. *Ibid.*, p. 308.
8. Sipri Year Book, 1969-70, pp. 239-40.
9. *Ibid.*,
10. Sidhu, K.S. "The Indian Ocean: A Zone of Peace; A study of India's Viewpoint", Harnam, New Delhi, 1983, p. 25.
11. Bull, Hedley "The Indian Ocean as a Zone of Peace" in T.T. Poulose *(ed.)* 'Indian Ocean Power Rivalry', Young Asia, New Delhi, 1974, p. 178.
12. Bull, Hedley "The Indian Ocean as a Zone of Peace", A paper presented in a Seminar on the Indian Ocean, New Delhi, 18-19 Feb. 1974, organised by JNU School of Int. Relations. Disarmament Studies Division.
13. Bannerji, B.N. "Indian Ocean: A Whirlpool of Unrest", Paribus, New York, 1984, p. 249.
14. Sidhu, K.S. *op. cit.*, p. 26.
15. The Working Paper submitted by Sri Lanka, "Calls for a gradual reduction and ultimate elimination of military presence of foreign powers from the Indian Ocean", Report of the Ad hoc Committee appointed by the UN General Assembly quoted in K.S. Sidhu, *op. cit.*, p. 33.

16. *Ibid.*
17. Subramaniam, K. and Anand, J.P. "Indian Ocean as an Area of Peace," India Quarterly, Vol. XXVII, No. 1, New Delhi, Oct-Dec. 1971.
18. Sidhu, K.S. *op. cit.*
19. Gupta, Inderjit "Peace and National Independence Threatened by Imperialist Bases in the Indian Ocean", on behalf of the Indian Government, in Seminar, *op. cit.*
20. Bull, Hedlley *op. cit.*
21. Position Paper of Sri Lanka, presented by MP Mr. Chandragunasekera.
22. Gupta, Inderjit, *op. cit.*
23. Bull, Hedlley *op. cit.*, pp. 181-186.
24. *Ibid.*, pp. 179-180.
25. Sidhu, K.S. *op. cit.*, pp. 34-35.
26. Gunasingham, C. "Indian Ocean: A Zone of Peace", Ceylon Daily News, 24 Feb. 1974, quoted in K.S. Sidhu, *op. cit.*
27. Simon, Sheldon V. "A Systems Approach to Security in the Indian Ocean Arch" ORBIS, Vol. XIV, No. 2, Philadelphia, Summer, 1970, p. 4064.
28. Kodikara, Shelton "An Area of Peace" Ceylon Daily News, 6 May 1975, quoted in K.S. Sidhu, *op. cit.*
29. Sidhu, K.S. *op. cit.*, p. 35.
30. Adie, W.A.C. "Oil Politics and Sea Power: The Indian Ocean Vortex", New York, 1975, p. 1.
31. Singh, K.R. "The Indian Ocean: Politics of Peace Zone" Akhatar Majeed (ed.) 'Indian Ocean Conflict and Regional Cooperation', ABC, New Delhi, 1986, pp. 138-43.
32. Singh, K.R. in Akhatar Majeed (ed.), *op. cit.*, pp. 135-36.
33. Singh, K.R. "Peace Zone How Relevant?" in "Indian Ocean and US Soviet Defence", C. Raja Mohan, K.R. Singh, Chandra, B. Khandun, V.D. Chopra, Michael Vlohas, T.R. Ford, (ed.), Patriot, New Delhi, 1991, p. 30.
34. Mishra, K.P. "Indian Ocean as a Zone of Peace: The Concept and Alternatives", India Quarterly Vol. XXXIII, Jan.-March 1977, No. 1, pp. 25-26.
35. Quoted in K.P. Mishra, *op. cit.*

36. Quoted in K.P. Mishra, "Quest for an International Order in the Indian Ocean", Allied, 1977, p. 97.
37. Quoted in *Ibid*.
38. *Ibid*.
39. *Ibid*.
40. Surahamanyam, K. "Confidence Building, Measures and Zone of Peace", Strategic Analysis, June 1989, Vol. XIII, No. III, pp. 255-56.
41. Bannerji, D. "Geopolitics of Peace in Indian Ocean Region" Strategic Analysis, Vol. 12, Nos. 1-6, 1988, pp. 27-28.
42. Position Paper of Sri Lanka, *op cit.*
43. Wriggins, Howard "The Indian Ocean Five Years Later" quoted in K.S. Sidhu, *op. cit.*
44. Namboodri, P.K.S. "The Indian Ocean: The Real Stakes" Strategic Analysis, Vol. II, No. 8, 1978, p. 312.
45. Wriggins, Howard, *op. cit.*
46. "The Iran-Iraq Conflict Testifies The Attitude of Regional Powers", cited in K.S. Sidhu, *op. cit.*, p. 71.
47. Bull, Hedlley "The Indian Ocean as a Zone of Peace", Seminar Paper, *op. cit.*

3

Indian Diplomacy

Diplomacy is a tool through which the goals of a nation's foreign policy can be achieved. India, in line with its democratic traditions, advocates and has adopted open and conference diplomacy. To achieve the goals of its Indian Ocean Policy also India has always emphasized use of international forums like United Nations and NAM.

India's perspective has evolved during the past four decades. From the non-alignment and peaceful-coexistence of the 1950's there emerged the concept of Collective Security in the region in 1960's which in 1970's assumed concrete conceptual framework in the form of the Indian Ocean as a Zone of Peace without shedding the concept of broad universal collective security or non-alignment.[1]

Important Planks on which India's Indian Ocean Policy is based are:

First, opposition to the big power military presence in the region–a "Peace Zone" strategy;

Second, improvement of her own image by removing misgivings about her Indian Ocean Policy, and

Last, promotion of regional consciousness, cooperation and community feeling among the Indian Ocean Countries and formation of an Indian Ocean Community.[2]

India's deep concern over the developments in the Indian Ocean and her vital commitment in favour of creation of a Peace Zone in Indian Ocean can only be understood when it is viewed in its proper historical and geographical perspectives; otherwise it is likely to be misinterpreted.[3]

Although many nations, both from within and outside the region, have an important interest in the Indian Ocean as a highway of international trade, none else, perhaps, is more vitally interested than India. For, while the shores of the countries of South Africa, Malaysia and Indonesia are washed also by the Pacific and Atlantic Oceans, and other African countries are mainly continental and the Persian Gulf region is more or less naturally a protected area, India is one of the four countries (Burma, Sri Lanka and Pakistan being the other three) which exclusively depend on the Indian Ocean.[4]

Geographically, India occupies a central position in the Indian Ocean, second only to Australia, having an area of 3,217,782 sq.km. surrounded by the Arabian Sea in the West, by the Bay of Bengal in the East and the Indian Ocean in the South. India has 6080 kms. of coastline with about 12000 islands and islets - 578 along the West coast including the Lakshadweep, Minicoy and Aminidive in the Arabian Sea and 667 along the East Coast in the Bay of Bengal including the Andaman and Nicobar Group.[5] Besides there are several artificial islands-oil and natural gas platform complexes on the continental shelf, as well as new emerging islands.[6] In addition to border security, India has all these strategic island possessions to defend, including the Andaman and Nicobar islands which are separated by over 700 nautical miles from the mainland.[7]

To India the security of this region is of paramount importance, as oceanic routes across this ocean carry the bulk of its overseas trade. As a developing country, with an ever-increasing industrial sector, India relies on the sea trade. India imports a large amount of petroleum, minerals, chemicals, hi-tech items and food. In return it is increasing its exports of numerous industrial and agricultural products including jute, tea, cotton, fabric, oil cake, leather products, cashews, fish and low-tech items. For this a secure sea-trade route is a must.

If these routes come under the influence of countries not friendly to India, this would very seriously threaten not only its economic and industrial development but also its very independence.[8]

India's maritime interests in the Indian Ocean can be summed up as follows:

1. Use of Sea for commerce and ensuring unhindered sea-borne trade.
2. Exploitation and protection of resources in its Exclusive Economic Zone (EEZ).
3. Exploitation of the high Seas and the Sea bed for living and non-living resources.
4. Research and development in the EEZ, high Seas and Antarctica.
5. Force projection.
6. Sea denial to adversaries, and
7. Defence of island territories.[9]

Historically, the Indian Ocean has played a vital role in India's national life from time immemorial. The rise and fall in her national life has been closely linked up with her maritime position. From the beginning of the Christian era till the advent of Europeans, India carried out intensive trade transactions with the countries around her in all directions. The decline of her naval power coupled with political disunity among the Indian rulers paved the way for long political subjugation by the Europeans. Thus in this particular geographical and historical setting, independent India has vital economic, political and security stakes in the Indian Ocean.[10]

India's Indian Ocean Policy in Pre-Independence Era

India was the first country of the Indian Ocean to possess real water fleets. In Chandra Gupta Maurya's times she had a board of Admirality with a superintendent of ships at its head. Later, in Akbar's days the Mughal navy had an impressive strength but during the later Mughals its strength dwindled and it could not succeed in standing upto the European powers navy in the Indian Ocean. The Marathas took a keen interest in developing a navy and troubled both the Mughals and the Portuguese on the Sea. Indeed, Kanoji Angre was the most dashing Sea Captain of his times. According to K.M. Pannikkar the control of the Indian waters remained in Indian hands even after the break-down of the Chola naval power, till the arrival of the Portuguese (the Arabs, who succeeded after the decline of the Chola naval power were only commercial navigators).[12] Within 15 years of the rounding of the Cape, the Portuguese were in control of all the key positions in the Indian Ocean, overcoming the strong joint resistance by the Arabs and Indians. Asia's supremacy came to an end towards the close of the 15th century. For the next 400 years, the history of the Indian Ocean was one of colonial rivalries and armed struggles among the western powers.

The Portuguese were followed (in the Indian Ocean) by the Dutch, the English, the Danes and the French. It was not until the consolidation of the British Power by the end of 18th century that any single power dominated the Indian Ocean. By 1900 the Indian Ocean was transformed into a British Lake with military control established over all important approaches and exits.[13]

As long as the Indian Ocean remained a British Lake, India perceived no threat to its interests from the residual British presence in Southeast Asia and the Middle East. Even when India opted out of Britain's imperial strategic system, it maintained close, political, economic and security links with the British. The British domination of the Indian Ocean permitted relative neglect of that body in India's strategic thinking.[14]

Panikkar aptly summed up the British domination of the Indian Ocean in these words,

"With her unchallenged supremacy in the Mediterranean and with the acquisition of authority over Egypt and the annexation of Cyprus, the Mediterranean route to India became a private subway for Britain with controls at different stages - Gibraltar, Malta, Port Said and Aden. The Red Sea became an exclusively British Sea lane, bolted and barred at both entrances, Aden assumed the importance it possessed during the time of Egyptian and Arabian navigation in the Indian Ocean, and it may well be said that the Suez Canal became, as events developed, the strongest link in the chain which bound India to Britain".[15]

Even when Britain began to weaken after first world war her naval dominance of the Indian Ocean continued for another 50 years ending formally with the "East of Suez" policy which marked the relinquishing of British control of the Indian Ocean, giving the final touch to the setting of the Sun on the British Empire. More than anything else, it was the British decision to withdraw militarily from the Indian Ocean which heightened the interests of both, the littoral States and the great powers, towards the ocean.[16]

1947 to 1965

For a long time the importance of the Indian Ocean for the security and commerce of India was not adequately recognized and most of the Indian historians remained preoccupied with the Himalayas and the landmass beyond the Hindukush on the Northwest. This northern bias of Indian historians was somewhat natural as, till the advent of the British, all foreign invaders had come from the Northwest direction through the mountain passes.[17]

Whatever the reasons, the apparent disregard of the sea-based danger is ironic in view of the fact that it was the sea that carried the forces that subjugated and occupied India for over two centuries. It was also apparent from World War II that the Ocean would play an increasingly vital role in the overall world security and that of the sub-continent in particular.[18]

India was perhaps initially lulled into belief at the time of her independence that her security depended on the good will and friendship of the neighbouring countries.[19] It failed to fully apprcciate that merely high moral values without a corresponding investment in national security was largely an exercise in wishful thinking, for as Ravindranath Tagore said, "Power has to be made secure not only against power but also against weakness."[20]

India rejected the instrument of balance of power and enwrapped itself in the cloak of non-alignment, relying on its immense dimensions, confident in its moral superiority, overestimating the role of the United Nations. It endeavored to provide an example, if not to the world at large, at least to the countries of Asia and Africa.[21]

K.M. Pannikkar was among the first Indians in post-independent India to call for a concerted policy by New Delhi towards the Indian Ocean. In his seminal work, "India and the Indian Ocean: An essay on the influence of sea power"[22], in 1945 he argued that **the Indian Ocean must remain truly Indian**. K.B. Vaidya echoed these very sentiments in 1947. In his book 'Naval Defence of India", he argued that, **"even if we do not rule the waves of all the five oceans of the world, we must at least rule the waves of the Indian Ocean."** The Indian Ocean can only be an "Indian Lake", according to Vaidya, if India is the supreme and undisputed power over the waters of the Indian Ocean.

An even clearer signal to India's future policy towards the Indian Ocean was manifested by a report of the study group of the Indian Council of World Affairs, which was released in 1957. The report argued that **the Indian Ocean was a "vital lake of the British Empire" and remains to be an important zone for the security of countries bordering it.**[24]

Three sides of India's frontiers are bordered by water; this cannot be lightly dismissed. India is progressively gaining ground as a coming Eastern Power. As such she has a big responsibility in taking active measures to remind her Asian neighbours of the need to provide jointly for the defence of this region, for their mutual security. Her resources in material and manpower could certainly contribute immensely to this task. India, though committed to a policy of non-alignment , cannot possibly neglect her seaward defences. She has unquestionably got to think of having adequate naval forces to protect the miles and miles of her coastline, even though by herself she cannot guard her sea trade communications alone. This can be done only by developing an understanding among the countries concerned and by their joint action.[25]

All these calls were unfortunately ignored and **India's Indian Ocean Policy from 1947 to 1965 can be justifiably described as to be one of "distance", "hands off", "evasionary" and at least "lackadaisical"** which can be explained by a number of factors:

First, the ongoing cold war with Pakistan as an American ally on the West of India and New Delhi's Policy posture of containing the so-called Pakistan threat ensured the neglect of the Southern interest.

Second, the looming China threat which manifested in the October 1962 war proved to the Indian strategic thinkers that their "northern bias" outlook was a correct one which forced them to exhaust their energies towards the north. If anything, it was their lack of depth and imagination of the northern threat that was blamed for India's humiliation in 1962.

Third, the fact that Britain was the dominant power in the region and had been so since 1815 provided the Indians with a sense of laxity, treating the Indian Ocean as a "British Lake" of their former "Sahibs" and from where no challenge was foreseen, and

Finally, in overall planning of immediate dangers, the threat from the Indian Ocean appeared least alluring and hence the continued neglect of the Indian Ocean as a security threat.[26]

This was evident in December 1973, following the US Seventh Fleet's entry into the Indian Ocean. Nehru's acceptance of it without any protest or fear reflected the Indian sense of security on the one hand and neglect on the other, more so, since this happened after the Sino-Indian war, where Americans had indirectly balked India.

Nehru's reaction to the Seventh fleet foray into the Indian Ocean was as follows:

If the US Government decides to do this (deploy in the Indian Ocean Region) all that we need say, today, is that outside the territorial waters of India, the ocean is, naturally, open to them, as to the naval vessels of any other country. [27]

All this was happening despite K.M. Pannikkar's highlighting the significance of the Indian Ocean for the security of India as early as 1944-45. Regretting the unfortunate tendency to overlook the sea in the discussions of India's defence problems he had remarked, **"India never lost her independence till she lost the command of the Sea in the first decade of the 16th Century".**[28]

1965-1971

A change in India's Indian Ocean policy and towards the Indian Ocean Region becomes perceptible from late 1965 onwards, mainly in reaction to the developments in the Indian Ocean Region.

However the Indian navy had remained the **"silent service"** and out of sight even during the Indo-Pak War of 1965. Policy makers on both sides, India as well as Pakistan, were "blissfully unmindful of the common denominator of the seas that joined the two segments of Pakistan with peninsular India being the bisector and hereby dominating the sea lanes of communication."[29] In this war both sides lacked the will to exploit the potential of sea power which had held the sub-continent captive for centuries. The major focus of this war remained on land frontiers once again establishing the fact that the "land oriented strategy[30] had correctly dominated India's defence policy. However the security of India has been time and again decided by the peace and stability of the waters that wash the three sides of the great subcontinent.[31]

This situation did not continue for long. Due to several reasons the Indian Government was forced to adopt a more clear-cut policy towards the region.

The Indian Government became more involved and concerned towards the developments in the Indian Ocean Region after the British declaration of its East of Suez Policy. "Initially India had welcomed Wilson's decision to withdraw British armed forces from the East of Suez, and had not perceived any vacuum created by the British withdrawal." At that time India had not expected Britain to invite the United States to build up a presence in the Indian Ocean.[32]

In October 1965, Wilson announced the establishment of a new geographical entity called "The British Indian Ocean Territory" (BIOT) consisting of a cluster of islands located between Mauritius and the Maldives. When it became apparent that the United States had been asked to build, "facilities" on one of these islands, Diego Garcia, India reacted with displeasure.[33]

On April 6, 1967, in the Lock Sabha debates the Minister of External Affairs, M.C. Chagla announced that "We are opposed to the establishment of military bases in the Indian Ocean Area, as it might lead to an increase in tensions in the region. We hope that, in the larger interests of peace, the British authorities will bear in mind our feelings and the feelings of other countries in this region and desist from setting up any military bases in this area."[34]

Although India made no formal protest to London and did not consult any of the littoral States, she played an active part in getting the United Nations Trusteeship Council to adopt a resolution condemning the British action and warning London that detachment of a part of Mauritius for the purpose of building an American naval base would amount to a contravention of the UN declaration on the granting of independence to colonial territories.[35] In the course of the year Mrs. Gandhi, the then Prime Minister of India, raised the idea of a possible Indian Ocean convention to ensure peace in the Indian Ocean Region but nothing developed further.

However, India categorically rejected the "vacuum" theory devised by the United States to establish herself in the Indian Ocean (in the wake of the British withdrawal according to its East of Suez Policy and establishment of BIOT) with the help of her allies. The Indian stand on the so-called "Vacuum" in the Indian Ocean was elaborated by Sardar Swaran Singh in the Lok Sabha on 10 April 1968. In his statement he said:

> "Government do not accept the validity of the propaganda that a vacuum will be created in the Indian Ocean on the British decision to withdraw from the areas East of Suez.... It is not our intention, firstly, to accept the validity of this concept that any vacuum can be created, if any foreign power leaves any particular area, then, it is for that area and for that territory to take adequate steps to safeguard their own security and their own country. If they ask any other country for help, that could be considered, but when even a country like the United Kingdom is withdrawing from overseas commitments, for a country like India, which has never believed in that concept, to think in these terms, is absolutely inconsistent, without approach to this problem.[36]

Again speaking on a call attention motion in the Rajya Sabha on 8 May 1969, on a statement by a naval study group at the Defense Services Staff College, Swaran Singh decried the talk about a "vacuum". He did not agree with the view that the British withdrawal from the Indian Ocean would affect India in anyway. He stated in the Rajya Sabha that, "**the British presence was not in our interest**"[37]. On another occasion, the then External Affairs Minister Dinesh Singh, in his speech on 8 April 1970 in the Lok Sabha called the British Navy, "**a symbol of domination in Asia**." He said, he was "**surprised**

and in many ways humiliated when my countrymen say what will happen if the British go away." He thus, welcomed the British withdrawal from the Indian Ocean as a process of decolonialization and expressed complete faith in the capacity of the New Asian Countries **"to meet the challenges that came with a measure of self-respect, dignity and self-reliance without looking to Washington or Moscow."**[38]

Inspite of all this on the question of establishment of bases in the Indian Ocean. India's stand, though one of opposition in general, was at times liable to be misunderstood, and left many things rather vague. When in July 1965, the Maldives gained independence, retention of the Gan base by the British evoked no protest from India whatsoever and later the same year when Britain and the United States began their preparations for setting up bases on the BIOT, there was no strong reaction in New Delhi, beyond a statement by Deputy Minister for External Affairs Dinesh Singh in the Rajya Sabha on a call attention motion by I.K. Gujral, which said that the Government of India's Policy in regard to bases in the Indian Ocean has been one of the strong opposition.[39] When members insisted on knowing about the specific steps taken to register protest at the international forum and to call a meeting of the affected countries, the Government only referred to the unanimous resolution passed at the Cairo Conference of the non-aligned countries condemning the setting up of bases in the Indian Ocean.

The ambiguity about the Indian Government's stand on Indian Ocean bases could not be fully dispelled. In the Lok Sabha debate foreign Minister M.C. Chagla, while monotonously repeated the Governments earlier statement that they were against any foreign military bases in the Indian Ocean, showed his readiness to accept the Anglo-American version that they were not establishing military bases. On 6 April 1967 Chagla Said, "All that we can do, for the time being, is to accept their statements that they do not propose to use those islands as military bases."

But these ambiguities were soon removed and vacillations overcome in time. The Indian Policy resumed its old initiative and drive. This reactivation of the old Indian stance against miniaturization of the zone of non-aligned nations and establishment of foreign bases became more noticeable from 1971 onwards.

1971 Onwards

For the first time in 1971, a land war acquired oceanic connotations. There were several engagements with Pakistan in the Arabian Sea and the deployment of units of the United States Seventh Fleet in the Bay of Bengal.[40]

This proved that the maritime strategy of a country is rooted in its national strategy, which, in turn, is dedicated to promoting and safeguarding its national interests. The National strategy is total in concept and has political and diplomatic, economic and commercial, cultural and geographical and military facts.[41]

India's national policy essentially supports:

1. Enhancement of its prestige and stature as a major Asian Power;
2. Promotion of commercial interests;
3. Reduction in influences of extra-regional countries;
4. Protection of Indian nationals in littoral countries, and the independence of other regional island nations;
5. Development of a major regional military capability to maintain mainland border security, and
6. to defend offshore under sea-bed resources, strategic insular territories and traversing Sea Lines of Communication (SLOC's).[42]

In this backdrop, India has been constantly concerned about its maritime security. Indian Ocean has occupied a focal position in India's foreign policy in view of its increasing militarization and nuclearization by the outside powers. The then Prime

Minister of India Mrs. Indira Gandhi speaking at the opening session of CHOGM on Sept. 4, 1980, said, "**the Ocean has brought consequences to India, in the past... Today we find it churning with danger... The frenetically increasing pace of militarization in the Indian Ocean makes the 3500 miles of our coast more vulnerable.**" Likewise Mr. Narasimha Rao the then External Affairs Minister reiterated in the Lok Sabha on April 3, 1981 that **India was deeply concerned over the happenings in the Indian Ocean, having grave implications for her security, as she was going to be the "first victim" if the Indian Ocean environment becomes polluted and vitiated.**[43]

India was among the 61 member states that voted for the proposal to declare the Indian Ocean as a Zone of Peace, but it neither openly took the initiative nor sponsored the original text, which was prepared by Sri Lanka and Tanzania. It became a cosponsor of the draft only at the first revision stage. The Indian Foreign Minister stated that India preferred to leave the initiative to the smaller countries of the region; may be, for the reason that an Indian initiative could arouse the suspicion in the minds of the neighbouring countries (moreover growing tensions in the then East Pakistan during that period might have worked as a constraint).[44]

The Indian stand can be described as correct, specially because India's concern and her active diplomatic efforts in the international field for the creation of a Peace Zone in the Indian Ocean have generally not been viewed in correct perspective by a number of foreign scholars and politicians. India's perceptions towards the Indian Ocean are considered as attempts to acquire a predominant position in the region. Their views are further substantiated by their referring to the writing of the great Indian Scholar Sardar K.M. Pannikkar, and the present day active interest exhibited by the Government of India with regard to the Indian Ocean.

But, such a viewpoint, as regards India's Indian Ocean Policy, seems to be biased as it ignores the imperatives of

India's maritime security. Against this backdrop India welcomed the attempt to involve the United Nations, as it suited the Indian approach perfectly well.

India sees the United Nations as an incomparable vehicle of communication and negotiation. There is perhaps no case more appropriate for the United Nations' consideration as the one under study. Given the fact of the formidable advantage the weak have in the world forum for articulating legitimate individual or group interests and grievances and also because the United Nations is an important forum for multilateral negotiations, India saw the initiative at the United Nations in 1971 as a welcome development. The object of the Ceylonese-Tanzanian initiative was no doubt ambitious, **"an international domain, subject to international regulation and responsibility, covering the entire high seas of the Indian Ocean."**[45]

The Afro-Asian bloc in the United Nations had begun mobilizing opinions regarding the Indian Ocean during the late 1960's and the early 1970's. These efforts of mobilization of opinions received an impetus soon after the formation of the base at Diego Garcia was announced.

In September 1971 fifty-four members of the non-aligned group met at the United Nations and decided on the concrete steps that should be taken to implement the Lusaka Declaration of a Peace Zone in the Indian Ocean. Following that, the delegate of Sri Lanka, Hamilton Shirley Amarsinghe, requested the Secretary-general on October 1, 1971 for the inclusion of the item on the agenda of the 28th session. Tanzania joined it as a co-sponsor on 7 Oct. 1971.

The plenary meeting of the General Assembly included the item on the agenda on 8th Oct. and the question was referred to the first committee. The resolution was put to vote in the first committee on 14 December 1971. Fifty members voted for the resolution, none against it and forty-nine abstained. It was a very narrow margin. The resolution was passed by the General Assembly without any change on

16 December 1971. Sixty-one members voted for the resolution, none against it and fifty-five abstained. (A/2832 XXVI, 16 December 1971, 2022nd Plen. Mtg.)[46]

On December 15, 1972, the General Assembly by a resolution (No. 2992 XXVII) decided to establish an Ad hoc Committee dealing with the Indian Ocean. It was decided that the committee should have no more than fifteen members. The terms of reference of the committee were limited to decide on the concept of the Indian Ocean as a Peace Zone and its implications. India was a member of this committee.

The objectives India has in the context of the Indian Ocean Security can now be crystallized as follows:

1. India's economic development, political stability and independence of action, should not, in any way, be affected by the possible actions in the Indian Ocean Region by the big powers.
2. India should aim to preclude or neutralize the impact of any whimsical or wayward action against it by the big powers.
3. Prevent big power rivalry in any part of the subcontinent. Despite Pakistan's pro-US stance and its inclusion in the United States CENTCOM it is still a non-aligned nation and India aims to keep it so.
4. To acquire such military capabilities as to inordinately raise the threshold of any big power military intervention in the South Asian Indian Ocean littoral.
5. Acquisition and deployment of Indian forces on island possessions to safeguard them from ownership disputes or hostile take-overs.
6. To help defend, if requested, the island republics in the Western Indian Ocean Region against mercenary or commando style invasion.
7. Prevent encroachment upon and protect the assets of the large Exclusive Economic Zone in the Indian Ocean Region.

These assets will cover the offshore oil deposits and the oil rigs, seabed, rare minerals, coastal monazite sands, fishery resources, etc.

8. Ensure the right to peaceful passage for naval units and the mercantile fleet in the Indian Ocean Region.

9. Ensure the safe passage to the scientific bases on the continent of Antarctica and at a later stage provide for the security of the base itself. With already two permanently staffed bases of Dakshin Gangotri and Maitri and the extensive satellite communication, weather charting and research facilities, India is already an accepted member of the Antarctic Treaty Parties Consultative Group.[47]

10. Protect commercial and economic assets even beyond the EEZ limits - such as the 150,000 Sq. mile area demarcated in the Indian Ocean Region for India to commence seabed mining operations as a **"Pioneer investor"**. India is only one of the six countries in the world and the first in the third world to have acquired this capability under the seabed treaty provisions of the UN conference on the law of the Sea.[48]

At present India is under a nuclear threat from the Indian Ocean front due to the deployment of the Great Powers sea-based nuclear weapons. To face a sea-borne nuclear threat to India's security at the diplomatic level there are three options before India:

1. to sign a joint naval defence pact in the Indian Ocean Region involving the Great Powers,
2. to acquire an independent nuclear deterrence, and
3. To continue the process of strengthening a "strategic consensus" against the presence of the Great Powers in the Indian Ocean Region.

In the final analysis, the first option is against India's non-aligned status, which has been a prominent feature in India's Foreign Policy ever since its independence. The second is also against India's declared policy of peaceful uses of nuclear energy and it will further nuclearise the Indian Ocean Region. Therefore, the last option, consistent with its policy of regional and global cooperation, would serve the security interests of the littoral and hinterland states of the Indian Ocean Region including India.

In this process, India's prime effort at the diplomatic level is to create a "strategic consensus" without the structure of a military alliance among the states of the Indian Ocean Region.[49]

Whatever motives and intentions might be attributed to India's high profile posture in the India Ocean. the fact remains that India has vital stakes in the Indian Ocean which warrant her attention at present as well as in the future. India has no other course to follow, but to work for the creation of a Peace Zone in the Indian Ocean. The deadlock in the United Nations on the question of implementation of the Peace Zone resolution and the inordinate delay has resulted in the loss of enthusiasm on the part of many littoral States. Though the creation of a Peace Zone in the Indian Ocean seems to be very difficult to achieve India has to continue her efforts for it.

After 1990

1990 proved to be a big watershed in world history. When nobody had expected or imagined, the USSR broke up, despite or may be due to, the process of privatization, liberalization and policy of openness. Anyhow, the sudden and unexpected fragmentation of the super power changed the security scenario of all the countries overnight. The USA became the sole super power with many big powers vying to take the place of the former USSR. Many new economic powers emerged to challenge the supremacy of the USA and the situation is best described as one of a 'uni-multipolar world.[50]

As a result of the break-up of the erstwhile USSR India lost a 'friend' and now had to concentrate on protecting its national interests in the era of globalization, privatization and liberalization with the help of new friends and new policies.

By this time the importance of the oceans for countries in general and that of the Indian Ocean for its littoral and specially for India, also had come to the fore front. Chinese, Japanese, Indonesian and French navies had started to make their presence felt and India had to review its policy options due to a variety of reasons e.g.

1. It was being pressurised to put its signature on the CTBT.
2. It had to exercise its option of testing nuclear devices in 1998 to qualify for a nuclear weapons state followed by Pakistan.
3. Ensuing economic sanctions by the USA were eye-openers for India's policy-makers.
4. Once again it was established by the behaviour the USA displayed in west Asia that the United Nations could not be very effective if it was not supported by the USA.
5. Non-traditional threats to the maritime security of India e.g. smuggling of drugs and human beings, piracy, pollution and terrorism had became more evident and prominent.
6. Even the USA realized (after Sep 11, 2002) that trying to fight terrorism and protecting its shipping single-handed was burdensome and sought India's help and cooperation in this regard.
7. In the changed circumstances India also agreed to enhance Indo-US cooperation to protect and further its national interests.

All these factors helped India to review its policy options and maritime policy and now it has begun to concentrate upon building its navy to make it a blue water navy. After the lost decade India increased its joint naval exercises in the Indian Ocean region with other countries including the USA.

References

1. Sidhu, K.S. "Indian Ocean: A Zone of Peace", Harnam, New Delhi, 1983, p. 85.

2. Mishra, R.N. "Indian Ocean and India's Security", Mittal, Delhi, 1986, p. 25.
3. Pathak, Saroj "India, South East Asia and the Indian Ocean", Strategic Analysis, April 1989, Vol. XIII, No. 1, p. 85.
4. Kaushik, Devendra "The Indian Ocean towards a Peace Zone", Vikas, New Delhi, 1972, p. 105.
5. Anand, J.P. "The Law of the Sea: India and the Indian Ocean", IDSA Journal, July-Sept., 1981, pp. 142-44.
6. Anand, J.P. "India's Islands and other Ocean Territories; Strategic Environment", Strategic Analysis, Vol. 12, Nos. 1-6, May 1988, p. 169.
7. Ford, Col. T.R. "Indian Ocean Demands More Attention", Strategic Digest, 1990, Vol. 20, No. 1-6.
8. Pradhan, Pradyot "Indian Ocean: Arena of Future Conflict:" Foreign Affairs Reports, 1988, March-April, Vol. 37, No's. 3-4, p. 15.
9. Rear Admiral Kohli, "India's Maritime and Geostrategic Interests in the Indian Ocean" in Satish Chandra, B. Arunachalam and V. Suryanarayan ed. "The Indian Ocean and its Islands, Strategic, Scientific and Historical Perspective" Sage, New Delhi, 1993, p. 66.
10. Pathak, Saroj *op. cit.*, pp. 87-88.
11. Pradyot, Pradhan, *op. cit.*, p.2.
12. Kaushik, D. "Perspectives on Security in Indian Ocean Region", 1987, pp. 10-11, Allied, New Delhi.
13. Choudhary, Niloufar "The Indian Ocean: A Zone of Peace and A Zone of Conflict", Asian Survey, April 1985, p. 250.
14. Gupta, Bhabani Sen "The View from India" in Abbas Amirie (ed.) "The Persian Gulf and Indian Ocean", Tehran, 1975.
15. Bezboruah, Monoranjan "US Strategy in the Indian Ocean: The International Response", Prager, USA, 1972.
16. Bilveer, Dr. S. "India and The Indian Ocean: As a Zone of Peace; From Neglect to Lackadasical Interest", Pt. I, Asian Defence Journal, Malaysia, Jan. 1990, pp. 18-19.
17. Kaushik, Devendra "Perspectives on Security in Indian Ocean Region", Allied, New Delhi, 1987, p. 108.
18. Bezboruah, Monoranjan, *op. cit.*, p. 192.

19. Vice Admiral (Retd.) M.K. Roy PVSM, AVSM, "Sea Power in the Indian Ocean" USI Journal, Delhi, Vol. XVII, NO. 493, July-Sept., 1988, p. 210-11.
20. *Ibid.*, p. 209.
21. Vali, F.A. *op. cit.*, p. 89.
22. Pannikkar, K.M. "The Strategic Problems of the Indian Ocean", Allahabad, 1944.
23. Vaidya, K.B. "The Naval Defence of India", Bombay, 1947, p. 91.
24. Cited in Defence and Security in the Indian Ocean Area: A Study Group of the Indian Council of World Affairs, New Delhi, 1957.
25. *Ibid.*
26. Bilveer, S. "India and the Indian Ocean As a Zone of Peace: Developing A Paranoid Obsession", Part II, Asian Defence Journal, Malaysia, Feb. 1990, pp. 33-37.
27. Lok Sabha Debates, Vol. 24, Col 5768, 19 Dec, 1963.
28. Pannikkar, K.M. "India and the Indian Ocean", *op. cit.*, p. 14.
29. Roy, Mihir K. *op. cit.*, pp. 46-47.
30. Sidhu, K.S. *op. cit.*, p. 72.
31. Pannikkar, K.M. "The Strategic Problems of the Indian Ocean", Allahabad, 1944, p.3
32. Gupta, Bhabani Sen, *op. cit.*, p. 187.
33. *Ibid.*
34. Kaushik, Devendra "The Indian Ocean: A Peace Zone", Vikas, New Delhi, 1972, p. 155.
35. Gupta, Bhabani Sen, *op. cit.*, p. 187.
36. Kaushik, Devendra "The Indian Ocean, A strategic Dimension", Vikas, New Delhi, 1985.
37. National Herald, 9 May 1969.
38. Lok Sabha Debates, Vol. 39, Cols. years 241-45.
39. Rajya Sabha Debates, Vol. 54, part I, 1965, Cols. 1915-22.
40. Gupta, Ranjan "The Indian Ocean: A Political Geography", Marwah, New Delhi, 1979, p. 72.
41. Kohli, S.N. "Sea Power and the Indian Ocean with Special Reference to India", Tata McGraw Hill, New Delhi, 1978, p. 105.

42. Bradley, Hahn "Sea Lanes Becoming More Vulnerable, More Important", Asia-Pacific Defence Reporter, Vol. XVII, No. 3, Sept., 1990, p. 10.
43. Quoted in Saroj Pathak, *op. cit.*, Govt. of India, Ministry of External Affairs, "India's views on the Indian Ocean", Jan. 1980-Oct. 1981, New Delhi, pp. 1, 16.
44. Murthy, C.S.R. "India and the Deadlocked Zone of Peace in the Indian Ocean", IDSA Journal, Vol. XVII, No. 1, July-Sept. 1984.
45. UN Doc. A/8492 and Add. 1, Oct., 1, 1971.
46. Singh, K.R. "The Indian Ocean: Big Power Presence and Local Response", Manohar, New Delhi, 1977, pp. 222-24.
47. Dharamrajan, Capt. H. "India's Role in the Context of Indian Ocean Security", USI Journal, Jan-Mar. 1990, Vol. CXX, No. 499, pp. 194-195.
48. Chandra, Satish, *op, cit.*, p. 67.
49. Singh, Satyavir. "Nuclear Threat to India, The Indian Ocean Front", Foreign Affairs Reports, Vol. XXXIV, No. 6, June 1990, p. 79.
50. Roy, Ash Narain, "For a Slice of Geopolitical Pie", Mainstream, Vol. XLII No. 48., Nov 20, 2004.

4

US Interests and Presence in the Indian Ocean

Britain's East of Suez policy shook the established balance of power in the Indian Ocean region and a new rivalry between the two super powers of the day began to dominate the region, which had far-reaching effects on the littoral and hinterland states of the Indian Ocean.

The United States was disturbed by the British decision to withdraw itself from the Indian Ocean region. It would have preferred a more muffled and qualified British announcement of withdrawal. The United State attitude on the question was summed up by Mr. Rusk at a news conference when he said," **It is known that many of us who have responsibilities (in Asia and South East Asia) have regretted the idea that there would be a significant British withdrawal from the Indian ocean.**[1]

The United States feared that there might emerge in the 1970's a regional grouping of Malaysia, Singapore and other countries of the Indian Ocean region, which had refused to join the SEATO. Moreover, it apprehended that once the British withdrew, the communist insurgency in the area, backed by the communist states, would pose a threat to the western interests. The British, however, took care to retain a foothold in the region even after they had withdrawn from it.

Britain retained a number of staying posts in the Indian Ocean even after her decision to withdraw from the East of Suez, apparently to counter the then Soviet presence. These ports included the Gan Island (Maldives Island), Masirah Island (Near Oman in the Arabian Sea), Bahrain Island (Persian Gulf), the Seychelles Group, Mauritius and Beira Patrol (Mozambique). The island bases from Mauritius and Seychelles were acquired and a new colony called the British Indian Ocean Territory (BIOT) was set up in the South West region of the Indian Ocean to construct defence facilities for the British and the Americans.

United States begins to take an interest in the Indian ocean

Apart from a relatively modest amount of trade with littoral nations of the Indian Ocean, the United State's interests did not really begin to grow until the late 1920's when the Americans put a foot inside the Middle Eastern Petroleum tent. From that moment onwards, the big American oil companies steadily expanded their holdings until they controlled nearly half the trade, including the enormous reserves in Saudi Arabia. As the United States commerce followed, the Americans became a familiar sight around the littoral. The United States military presence came later and can be said to have originated during the early days of World War II. Prior to that the appearance of a warship in the region was a rarity.[2]

In January 1948, the United States established the Middle East Force, limited over the ensuing years to a flagship and two destroyers. This politico-military symbol has operated ever since to show the littoral nations of the Indian ocean, Persian Gulf and Red Sea that the United States has a serious, albeit benign, interest in this region. Except for this, comparatively few Americans were involved in the deployment of the oil fields in the Gulf. Only a few in the United States paid any serious attention to the Indian Ocean.

At the beginning, the naval presence of the Untied States in the region was motivated partially by the erosion of British supremacy. As a super power with worldwide responsibilities, the United States wanted to restrict the expansion of Soviet power into the Indian Ocean.[3] But it was not the sole aim of the Untied States to fill up the so called power vacuum in the region.There were many reasons which caused the turmoil in this tranquilised sea.

Economic interests play a vital role in shaping US foreign policy, and a projection of American power and influence abroad is often rooted in economic necessity, in terms of an expanding economy for new markets and new resources for the U.S. Thus, economic considerations transformed the US quest for a strategy in the Indian Ocean from a purely military matter into a broad policy concern. The US economic interest in the Indian Ocean area continues on key resources and the transportation routes that we used to carry these resources to the west. The economic impact of the area on western societies was amply proved by the short oil embargo, following the Arab-Israeli war in 1973.

Apart from oil, US dependence on foreign sources of other raw materials was projected to increase considerably in the coming decades. Various factors have contributed to the United States' move from self-sufficiency in natural resources to the present stage of increasing dependence on imports in vital areas. Comparatively lesser costs of the foreign resources, the increasing use of alloy and other minerals that the United States cannot procure from domestic resources, and the consumer orientation of its economy provided an area of increasing US dependence on resources from foreign countries.[4]

During that period the Untied States felt that it had an interest in the stability and economic development of the countries in the region. It believed that instability and conflicts between regional powers, and a major change in the local balance of power would serve the interests of the Soviet Union or China and therefore would tilt the world military balance in its disfavour. In other words Washington considered that it is, generally speaking, in its interest to maintain the status quo; of course, a change of the status quo which would favour the allies or friends of the United States would not be irrelevant.[5]

This point of view was supported by some other writers too. They also stated that it was in its (the USA's) interest to uphold the statusquo. Since the early 1950's it has granted billions of dollars in economic and military aid to the littoral states, and United States involvement in the region was estimated to be well over 10,000 million dollars.[6] The US also had a historic interest in protecting the freedom of the ocean (20 per cent of world shipping occurs in the Indian Ocean). For strategic purposes, the northern areas of the ocean may be significant to it as launching zones for its ballistic missiles.[7]

Moreover, underwater long-range missiles have come to form the core of the United States' offence and defence strategy. America's primary strategic interests originate from the Poseidon-Trident submarines and the highly sophisticated communication system they need. Wherever there is an ocean there are freedom and manoeuvrebility, as well as secrecy and security, for nuclear submarines. The Indian Ocean would obviously be of utility in any offensive against the erstwhile Soviet Union, where industrial zones have been transferred inland for security purposes.[8]

Not only this, there is a new major development-discovery of a large concentration of strategic minerals on the ocean bed, particularly in the Indian Ocean. The polymetallic nodules found there contain manganese, nickel, cobalt, copper and many other minerals. A possible yield per square mile has been estimated at 30,000 tonnes of manganese, 36,000 tonnes of aluminum, 2,500 tonnes of cadmium, 17,000 tones of Iron, 400 tones of cobalt, 17,000 tones of nickel and, 650 tones of copper. Manganese alone, expected per square mile, is worth a million US dollars. Although the density of these minerals over the whole bed is not uniform, still there are over 47 thousand square miles in the Indian Ocean to exploit. This is enough to make moneybags made of multinationals.[9]

The exploitation of the seabed for minerals is already a reality. As early as in 1981 off-shore production of oil accounted for about 30% of the world's total output. Large gas deposits are still being exploited under the North Sea. Sea dredgers are mining gold, off-Alaska, diamonds off-Namibia, Titanium and Thorium are already being mined off Sri Lanka and Australia. Many of the sea metals are needed by the armament industries in the West. The US share of global consumption of minerals for military purposes is one-third of the total. It is, therefore, hardly surprising that the transnationals have already sunk billions in developing the under-sea mining technology, which involves very high expertise. The US manou on land or the sea have to be understood in this perspective.[10]

Thus, the goals of the United States Indian Ocean policy have been defined as "maintenance of sufficient military forces capabilities, rights and facilities to support the United States foreign policy strategy and economic interests.[11]

After the October 1973, Middle-East war and the associated oil embargo, the United States abandoned her policy of restrained military presence in the Indian Ocean. The Departments of State and Defence became conscious of the long-term strategic requirements of the United States in the Ocean. The United States aggressive strategy in this area was determined by the American debacle in Indo-China at the hands of the Vietnamese people, by the emergence of Bangladesh in 1971 and by the Arab oil embargo during the 1973 West Asia War.[12]

The United States entry into the Indian Ocean

In the wake of the British withdrawal to secure its interests in the area as a part of its global policy the Unites States entered the region.

It was reported in December 1963 that the USA had decided to send a part of its seventh fleet operating in the Pacific to the Indian Ocean. The official entry of the United States fleet in the Indian Ocean caused anxiety among some circles in India. Prime Minister Jawaharlal Nehru in a statement in the Lok Sabha on 19th December 1963 said, "All that we need to say today is that outside the territorial waters of India, the ocean is naturally open to them as to the naval vessels of any other country.[13]

It is still definitely not known whether the entry of the American fleet was an independent decision, or was related to the British policy of partial withdrawal from the "East of the Suez". There are, however, reasons to believe that Great Britain, the USA and Australia had chalked out a long term strategy, to regroup their forces from the littoral into the depth of the Indian Ocean, a retreat necessary in the light of the changing weapon system and the nature of the strategic deterrent posed by it.[14]

The United Kingdom in collusion with the U.S.A. decided in 1965 to establish British Indian Ocean Territory (BIOT). The BIOT consisted of Chagos Archipelago and the islands of Aldabra, Farquhar and Desroches. After grant of independence to the islands of Aldabra, Farquhar and Desroches in 1976, with Seychelles a now BIOT is limited only to the Chagos Archipelago.

In 1966, London and Washington had concluded a 50 years agreement involving the joint construction of a military communications facility in Diego Garcia, a coral atoll approximately one thousand miles South of India. In 1975, the United States Congress empowered the navy to construct a base and support facility there. Thus the United States has established the only Indian Ocean military base controlled by a super power. When completed Diego Garcia was expected to deal with as many as a dozen warships, including an aircraft carrier, all at once. A whole squadron of tactical jet fighters will be able to operate from there.[15]

United States Presence in the Indian Ocean

In the course of time the region has witnessed growing US presence in the area. In 1976 in addition to its island bases it was written that, "the United States is keeping a three-warship naval force comprising the command and communication ship La Salle (13,900 tons) and two destroyers in the Persion Gulf as a guest of the British navy. The command ship replaced the aging Valcour in July 1974. Some critics contend that the force is just visible enough to provoke trouble and too small to be of any consequence. This is not only the permanent Americal military force in the area, called the Middle East force, based at Bahrain since 1948. Besides United States navy warships have participated in the CENTO, SEATO and bilateral naval manoeuvres in the ocean since the mid-fifties and have paid good will visits to several ports on the periphery of the Indian Ocean".[16]

The United States began constructing a chain of communication stations and centres, of which the important ones are. Asmara (Ethiopla), Northwest Cape (along the coast of West Australia), a base near Peshawar (Pakistan, closed in 1969), Clark base and Subic naval station (the Philippines, now closed), seven bases at Utapao, Udoru, Korat, Dbol, Nakhon, Shamon, Takhil and Nom Phong (Thailand, 1972-73), Vacoas (Mauritius), a tracking station near Tananarive (Malagasy), a communication station at Mahe (Seychelles).[17]

In Australia its four major installations are located at Woomera, Pine Gap, Alice Springs and NorthWest Cape. Australia also had offered facilities to the United States and other allies at its newly constructed naval base at Cockborn Sound, near Perth, on the Southwest Coast of Western Australia.

The New US Bases

On 23 December 1977 the USA signed an agreement with the Ruler of Bahrain to use the former British naval base there to station its task force thus adding another naval base to its chain of bases in the Indian Ocean. The United States also set-up a communication station there. However, its latest and the most important base is considered to be Diego Garcia on which work had begun in March 1971.

With the reorganization of its naval commands in July 1971, the United States navy decided to step up its presence in the Indian Ocean. The Commander-in-Chief, of the Pacific

Command, based in Hawaii, was given control of the United States military operations, encompassing the entire Indian ocean from January 1971, thus effectively linking up an area stretching from the Western Pacific to South Asia, the Arabian sea and all the way to the South Atlantic.[18]

By 1st January 1976 eight task forces of the United States navy had visited the Indian Ocean. Their dates of entering the Indian Ocean are given below:

1.	Aircraft carrier	Hancock	(44,700 tons)	29.10.1973
2.	Aircraft carrier	Oriskany	(44,700 tons)	01.12.1973
3.	Aircraft carrier	Kitty Hawk	(80,000 tons)	11.03.1974
4.	Guided missile Cruiser	Chicago	(17,500 tons)	30.06.1974
5.	Aircraft Carrier	Constellation	(80,000 tons)	08.11.1974
6.	Nuclear Powered and nuclear powered missile cruiser long Beach	Carrier Enterprise	(89,600 tons) (17,300 tons)	11.01.1976
7.	Guided missile cruiser Reeves	(7,800 tons)	Mid July, 1975	
8.	Aircraft carrier a submarine, a destroyer, a frigate and a replenishment ship -	Midway	(5,100 tons),	2.10.1975.[19]

The United States suffered a set back in the Persian Gulf on 30th September 1975. A the request of the Bahrain government, the United States announced the phasing out of its Middle East naval force based on Bahrain. Barely a week after a SEATO ministerial meeting on 28th September 1975, the US decided to liquidate the 21 year old military alliance in a phased manner in two years in view of the changed circumstances in South-East Africa following the end of the Vietnam war and the emerging relationship between Peking and Washington. The strategic importance of the Bahrain naval base is stated to be considerable as it commands the waterway through which 800 million tons of oil moves annually.[20]

The reasons for the phasing out of the United States naval force were not spelt out. There can be three important factors involved in the decision:

1. It can be due to the Arab nation's reaction to the presence of the only foreign base in the midst of an oil rich region and pressure from the Arab, Asian countries for elimination of foreign bases set up in the Indian Ocean.
2. Iran which is determined to become the controlling force and plays a greater role in the region is building up and modernising its armed forces and will continue to do so in the next few years.
3. To fill the hypothetical "Power Vacuum," if any, the United States navy will continue sending naval task forces quite frequently to show the flag and protect United States' and its allies' interests.[21]

In continuance of this withdrawal policy of the United States we can see the announcement of President Carter on 9 March 1981 that, "he had proposed to the Soviet Union that the Indian Ocean become completely demilitarized. The declaration came as a surprise to many people in the United States Government. Pentagon officials at that time knew of no Presidential Review Memorandum (FRM) ordering a study of the question of arms limitations - naval or otherwise - in the Indian Ocean, nor were they aware that such an initiative was being contemplated.

Approximately one week after his initial announcement, in an address to the General Assembly of the United Nations, President Carter qualified his earlier reference to the demilitarization of the Indian Ocean. "We will... seek to establish soviet willingness to reach agreement with us on mutual military restraint in the Indian Ocean....." Subsequent statements did nothing to clarify exactly what aims the President had in mind for the Indian Ocean negotiations. Given these oscillating public pronouncements, those reasonably familiar with the vast region of the Indian Ocean, as well as the critical United States national interests and stakes in its waters and along its shores, can be forgiven for assuming that the president meant precisely what he had said in the first place, "complete demilitarization.[22] But with the coming in of Mr. Reagan's administration USA's defence budget immensely increased and the US policy changed due to the fast changing world scenario.

According to US analysts, the erstwhile Soviet Union had achieved strategic parity with their country and a powerful forward-deployed Soviet navy was challenging their fleets. "It uses these advantages whenever opportunities arise and the cost/benefit ratio seems favourable as it did in Afghanistan and according to the United States administration, is now doing in Poland". This military capability and the threat of intervention under advantageous circumstances are meant to serve:

1. to deter aggression against the USSR,
2. as a critical instrument of the Soviet foreign policy, and
3. as an instrument for preserving and expanding Soviet authority and influence in communist regimes and obtaining favourable relations with the new nations that emerge out of former colonial powers.

This capability also enables the Soviet Union to respond to actions by the United States, and the US allies and China perceived it detrimental to their interests.[23]

But, the United States enjoyed several major advantages over the then Soviet Union in the Indian Ocean region. It had not only several aircraft carriers, but also two important communication bases, in Australia and Diego Garcia. There had been no substantial evidence that the then Soviet Union was able to set up such communication facilities in the Indian Ocean. The then Soviet Navy, according to Washington information, could at the most utilize limited facilities in Marxist - South Yemen, which was in one corner of the Indian Ocean, whereas, the United States in collaboration with its friends had the opportunity to operate from several points throughout the Indian Ocean.[24]

The United States presence in the Indian Ocean was also accused of endangering the aspirations of the newly independent nations. For instance, in the Gulf region the then Soviet analysts saw these components of the military might of the United States at work (1) The United States military presence was exemplified in the naval force on permanent patrol in these waters, and (2) The rapid deployment force based in the United States military installations centred on Diego Garcia island, which according to them was a big Pentagon air and naval base.

After a period of the so-called détente and comparative peace the region once again witnessed enhanced US naval presence. On 1st January 1983 a new VI Command, the US Central Command (USCENTOM) was established. Its jurisdiction being Middle East, Pakistan, Afghanistan, Iran, Iraq, Jordan, the Arabian Peninsula, Saudi Arabia, UAE, Bahrain, Kuwait, Qatar, Oman, Yemen's, Kenya, Somalia, Djibouti, Ethiopia, the Sudan, Egypt and the Indian Ocean. Its Head Quarter is Florida.The other five Commands are -

1. Atlantic Command
2. European Command
3. Pacific Command
4. Readiness Command, and
5. Southern Command for Africa.

The establishment of the new VIth Command made it explicit that the region was once again becoming an area of crucial national interests for both the super powers. Not only the USA, but the erstwhile USSR was also trying to increase its naval presence in the Indian Ocean, effectively since 1968. Their moves and counter moves had become a threat to the independence and sovereignty of small and economically underdeveloped third world littoral nations of the Indian Ocean. The situation continued till the break-up of the former Soviet Union and the world being a unipolar world.

US presence in the Indian Ocean in the post cold war world

With the end of the Cold War and the disintegration of the erstwhile Soviet Union, the U.S. naval doctrine has undergone dramatic changes. The 1991 Gulf War changed the U.S. perception of threat from global threat to one of regional challenge and opportunities. The U.S. doctrine of fighting at high seas changed to one of power projection and of influencing events in the littoral regions such as the missile projection after the bombing of American embassies in Kenya and Tanzania. After the 9\11 attack on the U.S, the U.S. naval presence in the Indian Ocean is increasing constantly. The war against terrorism declared by the Bush administration established a new role for the naval forces and the need for regional allies and naval cooperation to fight terrorism.

The Navy Operational Concept of March 1997 stressed the U.S. ability to carry out swiftly and effectively any naval missions-joint or coalition-and to prevail decisively over any opposing force. While the Joint Vision 2010 of the armed forces provided the template for joint combat operations, the Cooperative Defence Initiative (CDI) of the Clinton administration in April 2000 embodies the U.S. strategy to consolidate its role in the Middle East through bases and extra military presence in the West Indian Ocean region. Admiral Vern Clark, Chief of naval operations, has outlined in 2002 the central tenets of the Vision. It divides the Navy's capabilities into three categories, Sea Strike, Sea Basing and Sea Shield. President Bush during his recent address at the U.S. Naval Academy said: "I am committed to building a future that is defined less by size and more by mobility and swiftness, one that is easier to deploy and sustain, one that relies more heavily on stealth, precision weaponry and technologies". Thus the U.S. Navy's strategic objective is to influence directly and decisively events ashore from the sea in the Indian Ocean Region (IOR).

The Indian Ocean Region, particularly the Middle East and Diego Garcia, are the only regions where the U.S. military and naval presence is growing in the post cold war era. The U.S. Fifth Fleet was recommissioned in July 1995, as a permanently deployed fleet for any part of the Indian Ocean, with a surveillance coverage of the Persian Gulf, the Arabian Sea and the western Indian Ocean. The significance of the Fifth Fleet is that it is the only component command of the Central Command that is Forward Deployed in its AOR (The Army, Airforce, Marine crops and Special Operations). The Fifth Fleet is the equivalent of the Sixth and Seventh Fleets of the U.S. Navy, composed of a CVBG (an aircraft carrier, four principal surface combatants, two nuclear powered submarines and a support ship and an ARG and MEF).[25] Thus on the average its commander has some 15-35 major warships under his operational command at any given time.[26] The Fleet acts as an amphibious task force, commanding landing forces as well as provisions for multiple carrier battle groups in several locations. The increased tension in the regions invariably results in multinational naval and military force levels as seen during the *Operation Enduring Freedom* campaign against Afghanistan and the latest war on Iraq. By 1998 there were 19 combat warships, 300 aircraft and more than 24,000 troops deployed in the area, with 21,700 American and British naval and marine personnel and nearly 8000 airmen.[27] The presence of the U.S. warships like USS COWPENS, USS SHILOH (cruisers), USS BRISCOE, USS ELLIOT, USS HAYLER, USS MILIUS (destroyers), USS COLOMBIA (a nuclear powered submarine and, U.S. TOMAHOWK SLCMs clearly demonstrates the ability of the U.S. Navy to exercise power against littoral states deep into the hinterland from the sea and its capacity for forward deployed naval forces far from home bases in the U.S.[28] Geo-politically speaking, the Fifth Fleet's regional role is complemented by the fact that many of the regional states in IOR, especially those in the Middle East, are virtual U.S. protectorates. The U.S. thus provides naval security to Saudi Arabia, Kuwait, Bahrain, Oman, the UAE, Jordan and Israel. Regional states that oppose the American role are subjects of littoral attack (Iraq), moral vilification (Iran) and economic and other sanctions (Syria, Libya and the Sudan).[29] The U.S. interest in this region, of course, is oil as the gulf region consists of 60% of the world's proven oil reserves.[30] The Persion Gulf and Russia in the foreseeable future will be the biggest reservoirs of oil,[31] while the Central Asian Republics, Kazakisthan, Turkmenistan and Uzbekisthan are said to posses more than 25 billion barrels of proven oil reserves and at least seven billion cubic meters of natural gas reserves.[32] Thus the strategic objective of the U.S. in this part of the Indian Ocean is to maintain its control over the oil resources of the Gulf region, to protect the sea lanes of communications, to safeguard the passes of oil imports and exports of its allies and extend its military influence into the heart of Central Asia, particularly Uzbekisthan and Tazikistan.[33]

The campaign against the *Al Qaida* terrorist group by the U.S. led alliance made the region more vulnerable to external surveillance and extra-regional intervention in the name of countering terrorism, more so as the Bush Doctrine proclaimed Asia as an 'Axis of Evil' whose contours stretch from the gulf through the Malacca to Vladivostok. The extended goal of the U.S. naval strategy in the western flank of Indian Ocean is to keep Russia weak and subdued and keep the so-called rogue Islamic states like Iran and Iraq contained. On the eastern flank of the Indian Ocean China's military modernization and projection of blue water naval objective by 2020, raise serious security concerns among the U.S. allies in the Eastern Hemisphere. China has not hesitated to use force in the South China Sea and is making enough advances into the Indian Ocean.[34] To safeguard her regional interests the US has thus acquired strategic facilities and bases in countries like Bahrain, Kuwait, Oman, Qatar, Saudi Arabia and the UAE. In the eastern Indian Ocean the U.S. dependable allies are Singapore, Thailand and Australia. Diego Garcia in the central Indian Ocean, of course, is the key naval base in the region whose strategic advantage was proved in the campaign against Afghanistan. While the rogue states doctrine provided the U.S. with the *raison d'être* for global domination, it has also impinged on her the need to fight war with two rogue states simultaneously as required.[35]

US interest in the Indian Ocean: A change in perception

At a time when the cold war was at its height both the super powers, the USA and the USSR, were very strong (or apparently so) and nobody had expected or even imagined when the unthinkable and unimaginable happened-the Soviet Union broke up. Whatever the reasons behind the disintegration of the former USSR (here we are not concerned with them), the fact was that everybody was taken aback by this development, including the United States of America. No nation was prepared to deal with the situation that had developed after about half a century of stiff competition. The USA was left alone without a serious contender who would pose a challenge to its supremacy.

In this changed scenario like many other nations, the United States also had to review its foreign policy and relations with other countries including the littoral nations of the Indian Ocean. It had to redefine its national policy in many spheres including the Indian Ocean. In addition to the disintegration of the Soviet Union at this very time, many new developments were taking place at the international level. Southeast Asian countries as a group had become very strong economically and were challenging the US superiority in the region. They had become a force to reckon with in the form of Asian Tigers.

China was rapidly progressing economically, was gripping the world markets/ economy with its less expensive products in addition to modernizing its navy and making its presence felt in the Indian ocean, especially in the South China sea.

Many new centres of power like Japan, Germany and the European Union emerged converting the uni-polar world into a multi-polar world.

And to top it all, in the changed world circumstances India too decided to exercise its nuclear options in mid 1998. Now it made it clear that instead of using nuclear power only for peaceful purposes it was ready to use it for its defence if the need ever arose. As was to be expected India was followed by Pakistan immediately thus bringing the nuclear arms race to the very centre of the Indian Ocean.

By this time the importance of the oceans, their maritime resources and the Sea-lanes of communication (SLOC'S) were established beyond doubt.

The terrorist attacks on the Twin Towers of New York, came as a shock and now the super power realized that even its own security was not fool-proof. It also created terror in the minds of American policy makers about a possible terrorist attack on its territory from the sea front. This brought to the fore the need to secure its maritime trade, specially the oil imports through the Indian Ocean that has to pass through the terrorist/ pirate infested Malacca straits. After some terrorist attacks on merchant shipping the USA was forced to seek the cooperation of regional countries to protect its own vessels and called for joint naval exercises, escorting and patrolling of piracy prone areas with regional countries like India and Singapore. Both these countries, as opposed to other regional countries agreed for enhanced naval cooperation with the Untied States despite protests from within and by other regional countries. Hence in the contemporary times the objective of the USA is to protect its own national and maritime interests in the Indian Ocean. For this it had to eat humble pie too e.g., lifting economic sanctions from India which had come into force due to its nuclear explosions in May 1998.

References

1. Bhasin, V.K., "Super Power Rivalry in the Indian Ocean", S. Chand and Company, New Delhi, 1981, pp. 26-27.
2. Hanks, Robert T., "The Indian Ocean Negotiations; Rocks and Shoals", Strategic Digest. September 1978, Vol. 8 No. 9, p. 28.
3. Shah, Zafar, M.A. "India and the Super Powers: India's Political Relations with the Super Power" in 1970's, Dhaka, Bangladesh, 1983, pp. 113-114.
4. Bannerjee, B.N., "Indian Ocean, A Whirlpool of Unrest", Paribus Publisher, New Delhi, 1984. pp. 233-234.
5. Bannerjee, B.N. *Ibid*., pp. 236-237.
6. Bezbourah, M. "US Strategy in the Indian Ocean: The International Response", New York, Prager, 1977, p. 43.

7. Vali, F.A., "Politics of the Indian Ocean Region: The Balance of Power", The Free Press, New York, 1976, p.185.
8. Shah, Zafar, M.A., *op. cit.* pp. 114-115.
9. Bannerjee, B.N., *op. cit.* pp. 237-238
10. *Ibid.*
11. Kaushik, Devendra, "Super Powers in the Indian Ocean", Political Science Review, Vol. 10, No. 3-4, July-December 1971, p.81.
12. Bhasin, V.K., *op. cit.*
13. Sin, K.R., *op. cit.* p. 24.
14. Sin, K.R., *op. cit.* pp. 28-29.
15. Shah, Zafar, M.A., *op. cit.* pp. 114-115.
16. Anand, J.P., "Big Powers and the Indian Ocean", IDSA Journal, Vol. III, No. 4, April-June 1976, p. 581.
17. *Ibid.* pp 581-582.
18. Manning, Robert, "US Presence in Indian Ocean", The Times of India, 1 December 1975.
19. IDSA News Review on South Asia, November 1975, pp. 1139-40.
20. Anand, J.P., "Bahrain Naval Base", IDSA News Review on South Asia, October 1975, pp. 945.
21. Anand, J.P., "Big Powers and the Indian Ocean, "IDSA Journal 1976, *op. cit.* p. 590.
22. Hanks, Robert T., "The Indian Ocean Negotiations, Rocks and Shoals", Strategic Digest, September 1978, Vol. 8, No. 9, p.25.
23. Jhaveri, Satyavati S., "Super Power Rivalry in the Indian Ocean", Foreign Affairs Reports, Vol. XXVI, No.2, February 1982, p.30.
24. Sin, K.R. *op. cit.* p.182
25. See. Rahul Roy Choudhary, "U.S. Naval Policy in the Indian Ocean", *Strategic Analysis*, December 1991, p.1.
26. *Ibid.*
27. *Defence News*, February 2-8, 1998, pp.3 and 20.
28. *Ibid.*, see also http://www.198.80.36.9\ndu\inss\strtforum\forum98.html.
29. Adam, Garfinkle, "Agenda 2000- The U.S. Imperial posture in the Middle East", Orbis, Vol-41, no.1, Winter 1997, p-16.

30. See Mahapatra, "The Major Post Cold War Trends in India's Neighbourhood," *Strategic Analysis*, June 1999, p.386.
31. Mohan, C. Raja, "Geopolitics and Energy Security", *Strategic Analysis*, December 1996, p.1271.
32. *Ibid*.
33. Muni, S.D. "The Emerging Cold War in Asia: India's Option," *Strategic Analysis*, Vol. 19, no-12, March 1997, p.1603. See also Nayan Chanda's report "Long Shadow" in, *Far Eastern Economic Review*, December 28 and January 4, 1996.
34. *Ibid*., no.-7, p-144
35. *Ibid*.

5

Littoral States and Sea Politics

Which countries belong or should belong to the Indian Ocean region is a subject of controversy. The coastal countries naturally belong to the area; it is only the countries of the hinterland about which there is a difference of opinion. In this respect a sound principle which needs to be accepted is that all those countries which are located in the immediate hinterland, which are land-locked and whose vital interests are inextricably interwoven with the Indian Ocean, belong to this area.

This criterion seems to have been widely accepted in the discussions within the United Nations. According to the UN classification, the hinterland countries of the Indian ocean region are those countries which have access to the Indian Ocean only via the coastal states and whose security is affected by developments in these states. The region thus defined includes a large number of countries spread over three continents namely:

1. Afghanistan
2. Australia
3. Bahrain
4. Bangladesh
5. Bhutan
6. Botswana
7. Burma
8. Burundi
9. Comoros
10. Djibouti
11. Egypt
12. Ethiopia
13. India
14. Indonesia

15. Iran
16. Iraq
17. Israel
18. Jordan
19. Kenya
20. Kuwait
21. Lesotho
22. Madagascar
23. Malawi
24. Malaysia
25. Maldives
26. Mauritius
27. Mozambique
28. Nepal
29. Oman
30. Pakistan
31. Qatar
32. Rawanda
33. Seychelles
34. Singapore
35. Somalia
36. South Africa
37. Sri Lanka
38. Sudan
39. Swaziland
40. Thailand
41. Uganda
42. United Arab Emirates
43. United Republic of Tanzania
44. North Yemen
45. South Yemen
46. Zimbabwe[1]

All these countries together constitute approximately one third of the international comity of nations, belonging to three continents i.e. Asia, Africa and Australia.

Due to their ethnic, socio-economic and cultural diversity, the coastal, hinterland and island states of the Indian Ocean Region do not permit a clear-cut sub-division of the region which is essential to carry out a systematic study of the Indian Ocean region.

The seven sub-regions scheme given by Dieter Braun is a successful attempt to provide a basis on which a systematic study of the Indian Ocean Region can be carried out. The scheme is as follows:

1. South and Eastern Africa
2. Islands and Groups of Islands in the Western Indian Ocean
3. The Horn of Africa and the Red Sea
4. The Persian Gulf
5. South Asia
6. South East Asia
7. Australia[2]

A further division on the basis of their reaction to the UN resolution puts the littoral and hinterland states of the Indian Ocean Region into four categories:

1. Those who extended unqualified support and voted in favour i.e. Sri Lanka – Sponsor, Tanzania – Co-sponsor, Kenya, India & Malaysia.
2. Those who accepted the Peace Zone resolution. Only in principle and voted in favour i.e., Afghanistan, Tunisia, Pakistan, Iran & Indonesia.
3. Those who did not express themselves either way but voted in favour i.e. Somalia, Sudan, Swaziland, Yemen, Zambia, Bhutan, Egypt, Nepal, Qatar, Iraq, Kuwait, Uganda, and
4. Those who expressed misgivings about the soundness of the proposal and abstained from voting i.e. Australia, Madagascar, Thailand and Singapore[4].

1. South and Eastern Africa

South Africa is strategically located between the South Atlantic and the Indian Ocean. Its strategic significance is due to its very efficient ports on the Indian Ocean and its surveillance capacity in the Cape. The strategic significance of South Africa will continue to remain inspite of the dramatic end to the cold war and the dissolution of the Soviet Union.

Since the Republic of South Africa is endowed with minerals that are used in the defence industries of Europe and the United

States of America, there will always remain an interest in the West for South Africa's survival in a manner that will continue to provide an uninterrupted supply of minerals.

Today, the successor state of the Soviet Union, Russia maintains diplomatic relations with Pretoria, thus rendering previous analyses, evolved in a bipolar world, defunct.

The Indian Ocean with its critical strategic zone along the western littoral is the vital variable in South Africa's developing hemispheric strategy. The United States of America, the only Super Power has, not accepted the concept of the Indian Ocean as a Zone of Peace, as yet in the post cold war era. Apart from the strategic importance attached to the Indian Ocean by the United States there are a number of other factors that explain its priority. Consistent with a growing global trend, the European share of South Africa's total trade is declining whilst Asia's share is growing rapidly. Japan is presently, Pretoria's second largest trading partner after the United States.

It has been widely recognized that the Indian Ocean offers to the United States, the power to dominate the rimland of Africa, the Middle East and the Indian subcontinent, and dominance of these states can be achieved by a maritime strategy. In this sense, the Cape of Good Hope is the principal maritime entry arena to the Indian Ocean.

The Republic of South Africa provides a main base without a parallel in the Southern Hemisphere.

2. Islands and groups of islands

After the closure of the Suez Canal in June 1967, the geostrategic position of Mauritius, lying off the eastern coast of Africa, aroused interest in maritime power. The island has since become prominent in international commerce because of the intensive use of the Cape Sea route and the consequent increase in maritime activity at Port Louis. Its closeness to the world's most important oil tanker lanes and the West Asian oil fields has added to its strategic value. The reopening of the Suez Canal in 1975 has not diminished its importance. Port Louis is also a port of call for expeditions to Antarctica.

The Americans were granted facilities including a satellite tracking station at Vacoas and landing rights for military aircrafts. US aircrafts from Diego Garcia have been using the airport frequently.

Mauritius has been demanding the return of Diego Garcia, which was taken away from it by the Untied Kingdom before granting it independence in 1968 and was leased to the United States of America.

The Mauritian Government calls the US military presence a threat to regional peace and security and wants to keep all the big powers out of the Indian Ocean. Mauritius is committed to complete demilitarization of the Indian Ocean. India has reiterated its full support for Mauritius' sovereignty over the Chagos archipelago, which includes the Diego Garcia atoll.

Addressing the non-aligned nations, summit in New Delhi on March 8, 1983, Jugnath demanded that the island of Diego Garcia should immediately be returned to Mauritius and big power activities in the Indian Ocean should cease. The US base, he said, posed a constant threat to the security of his country and all the littoral states of the Indian Ocean. The summit in its declaration expressed full support for Mauritius over the Chagos archipelago including Diego Garcia and called for its early return to Mauritius.[5]

The Mauritian Prime Minister, Aneeroodh Jugnath, who had taken over on June 17, 1982, declared his country's unflinching dedication to complete demilitarization of the Indian Ocean in pursuit of its non-aligned policy. He expressed grave concern over the continued military presence of the Super Powers in the Indian Ocean. He wanted the Super Powers to move out of the Indian Ocean.

3. The Persian Gulf

Iran regards her Indian Ocean role as an extension of her role in the Gulf. Her rapid naval deployment along very sophisticated lines indicates her determination to be a strong and dominant Indian Ocean power. While her land forces could be involved in border defence or some border policing, it is the ocean that is given prime importance in her defence blueprints because her life blood-her trade – depends on it.[6]

The evaluation of Iran's Ocean role falls in three broad phases – **First,** up to 1967, when Iran like any other state of the Persian Gulf was an on-looker, withdrawn inwards to its geographical core. **Second,** from 1964 to 1971, the period when Iran took effective measures to establish its supremacy in the wake of the British withdrawal from the Gulf. **Third,** Since 1972, when Iran's Persian Gulf role impelled it to declare openly Iran as an Indian Ocean power.[7] Vast reserves of oil in the Gulf have increased the importance of the Gulf countries immensely.

4. South Asia- India, Pakistan, Maldives and Nepal

The countries of South Asia, with the largest concentration of people, can be considered the **epicentre** of the Indian Ocean Region. But they are faced with the dilemma of having relatively little influence in shaping, and even less control over, the situation in the Ocean on which they heavily depend economically as well as strategically. If oceanic access to their shores is jeopardised or curtailed or if the Indian Ocean comes under the control of a hostile power/ powers their maritime vulnerability would become apparent. Although their foreign policy experience and orientation differ in many respects, the South Asian states have certain common interests and approaches to the Indian Ocean affairs. Their main objective is to keep the Indian Ocean an open sea without threats to their access routes or to their maritime interests. They want the Indian Ocean Region to remain a Zone of Peace rather than an area of great power rivalry and confrontation.

India

The Indian Ocean has been named after the land which projects towards the centre of the ocean for fifteen hundred miles. This strategic location enables a power based on the subcontinent to control the ocean with minimal forces. The reverse also is true; any power which is able to control the major trade routes of the ocean, will control "India's destiny,"[8] specially so because the Indian subcontinent has a coast line as long as, and more vulnerable than, the Indian land frontier and the largest in the world facing navigable waters.

The importance of the Indian Ocean for India cannot be over-emphasised as its physical configuration brings approximately 50 per cent of the Indian ocean within a thousand mile arch ascribed from the Indian territory. On the positive side, it means that the country has acquired one of the largest exclusive economic zones (EEZ) in the world (approximately two million square kilometres) inclusive of the sea around its island territories. In a strategic context, the implication is that with the appropriate weapons system, land-based military power can be projected from and integrated with India's sea-based capability over a wide swath of the Indian Ocean. On the negative side the country has that many more economic assets to patrol and protect and is that much more exposed to physical ingress along its long coastline.[9]

Still, scant attention was paid to the Indian Ocean in the two decades following independence because the leaders of the independence movement in India were concentrating on the expulsion of the British from the subcontinent and on attaining political freedom in their own land. After independence too they inherited the defence problems that the British had faced and adopted the same defence strategy. Their attention like that of the British was focused on the land and not the oceanic frontiers.

The only prominent Indian who tried to overcome the neglect of oceanic factors in India's defence was Sardar K.M.

Panikkar, who even before the independence was writing voluminously on strategic problems in the Indian Ocean and on the importance of the Indian Ocean to India's future. But, almost no one else of any influence gave much recognition to the importance of Indian Ocean. In the 1950's a study group organised by the Indian Council of World Affairs discussed the problems of defence and security in the Indian Ocean and issued a brief report in 1957, but apparently this attracted little attention. India's planning made little provision for ocean defence.[10]

It was the Bangladesh Liberation War of 1971 and the Oil embargo by the Middle East countries in 1973-74 together with the subsequent developments that brought the strategic importance of the region to the forefront and forced India to revise its policy towards the Indian Ocean Region.

India being the strongest and largest country of the Indian Ocean Region feels that it is only essential for the effective execution of its policy of non-alignment but also to its (and of other littoral states too) national interest that the Indian Ocean be made a Zone of Peace.

India believes that the responsibility of the security of the Indian Ocean should belong chiefly to the littoral countries and that the naval presence in the region of any external power is unacceptable. As early as 1965, India's deputy minister for external affairs said that the Indian Government completely opposed construction of foreign bases in the Ocean.[11]

India values her independence and is determined to stand her ground. Whatever the obstacles India, whilst concerned over the defence of her maritime interests, has no desire to extend a predominant influence in the Indian Ocean or play the maritime gendarme. She opposes the concept of any power or constellation of powers dominating it, to the detriment of others and will adamantly strive for universal acceptance for the Zone of Peace concept.[12]

Pakistan

The Indian Ocean washes about 600 miles of Pakistani shores. Pakistan's bulk of foreign trade moves by sea. About 85 per cent of her oil comes from the Gulf and among her vital imports are ferrous and non-ferrous metals and machinery of all kinds. So, its economic interests are involved in the Indian Ocean Rgion.[13]

As regards its strategic interests, the history of Pakistan's relations with India needs no elaboration. **"What displeases India, pleases Pakistan"**. India is perceived as the main threat to Pakistan's Security.[14]

Pakistan's attitude towards the Indian Ocean can be said to have two aspects-psychological and substantial. It has proposed quite a few times that the ocean's name should be changed as it gives undue importance to India.

Latif Ahmed Sherwani, a scholar from Pakistan's Institute of International Affairs, Karachi, read a paper at a conference on "The Indian Ocean" organized by the George Tow University's Centre for Strategic and International Studies in 1971, making out a case for calling the Indian Ocean by another name.

He suggested that it should be called "The Eastern Ocean" or "the Afro-Asian Ocean". The name Afro-Asian Ocean would be more appropriate as it washes the coasts of Australia and many other countries in Asia and Africa.[15]

Pakistan has always emphasised on limiting the big as well as the regional powers' (i.e. India) influence in the Indian Ocean. Though it has supported the Indian Ocean Peace Zone proposal, "The support is more superficial than real."

Though Pakistan voted for the General Assembly resolution of December 16, 1971 on Declaration of the Indian Ocean as a Zone of Peace and it was also included as a member of the 15-nation Ad hoc Committee set up by the UN General Assembly to suggest political measures to promote the concept of a Peace Zone in the Indian Ocean, it has always been partial in its politics. It has denounced the Big Power presence in the Indian Ocean but in doing so, it always pointed at the former Soviet Union and ignored the activities of the USA. As for the regional powers it has always demanded a curtailment of India's power but has comfortably ignored Indonesia and Iran's increasing naval presence and influence. More recently it has welcomed Chinese presence in the region and is trying to make its own presence, in the ocean felt at the international level by establishing Gwadar base. Not only this Pakistan demanded an active role for CENTO in the region, which shows that its support to this concept is formal and superficial.

Maldives

Maldives gained strategic significance primarily because a Rapid Advance Force (RAF) staging post was located on the island of Gan, situated in the centre of the Indian Ocean. The island lies close to the maritime routes from the Red Sea, the Arabian Sea, the Persian Gulf and the East African ports to the Malacca straits and the Far East. Its closeness to the world's most important oil fields has added to its strategic value.

Conscious of its geostrategic importance and the vulnerability of being drawn into the big-power rivalry, the Maldivian leaders feel that the best chance of the nascent nation (full independence granted in 1965) retaining its entity is by steering clear of entanglements with the big powers, while maintaining friendly relations with them.

A member of the non-aligned group, the Maldives has consistently supported the moves for making the Indian Ocean a Zone of Peace in the face of considerable pressure from some of the big powers to give them access to the Gan vacated by Britain in 1976. But, it has also failed to formally oppose Russian or American naval activity.

Bhutan and Nepal

Isolation from the outside world has characterized Bhutan's position. It was as early as 1910 that Bhutan signed an agreement with Britain under which the country's foreign relations were to be "guided" by the advice of the Viceroy of India representing the Crown. When India became independent a new treaty was agreed upon in 1949. New Delhi continued to guide Bhutan in its foreign relations. With the consent of India, Bhutan applied for membership in the United Nations and was admitted in 1971. Except for the Indian representative, there are no diplomatic missions in Thimpu.[16]

Bhutan's international status is somewhat anomalous. She is an independent state but dependent on "India's advice" in foreign relations and without direct external contracts except a permanent mission in the United Nations.

Since 1951, Nepal's foreign policy has been officially guided by the principle of non-alignment. It is remote from the Indian Ocean but its geographic location confers significance to its position in relation to the power balance in the Indian Ocean Region. It has always voted in favour of the Indian Ocean Peace Zone proposal.[17] But, the situation is changing fast now. Nepal is showing signs of coming closer to China and appears to be distancing itself from India. This is evident from the bloody killings of the Royal family in Nepal, its increasing differences with India and now from the new and ongoing constitutional problems. It is very difficult to predict at this stage whether Nepal would continue to support India or will take the side of China in times to come.

5. South-East Asian States - Indonesia, Malaysia, Singapore and Burma

The ASEAN countries occupy an important place in the vast littoral region of the Indian Ocean. Developments of the past 20 years are of critical significance to them, as they can have an adverse effect on their immediate security environment.

Except Burma all ASEAN countries are also Pacific Ocean countries. The narrow straits of South East Asia provide a link between the two oceans, as well as the two worlds - the East and the West.

Though the ASEAN countries support the proposal for establishing a Peace-Zone in the Indian Ocean, there are striking differences in their individual viewpoints regarding its desirability and feasibility which should be viewed in the context of their national interests and security threat perceptions.

Indonesia

As an Indian Ocean nation which has a long coastline stretching from North Sumatra to Timor, Indonesia displays a deep consciousness about it.[18]

President Sukarno went so far as to declare that the Indian Ocean should henceforth be known as the **"Indonesian Ocean"**[19] and for a few years the new name was in common usage in Jakarta.

President Sukarno in an address to the first National Maritime Assembly, thus described his country's mythology about the Indian Ocean:

> "Ever since the second Mataram Kingdom it is said that a King, a country, can only be peaceful and great when he is married to Queen Loro Kidul, who ruled the Indonesian Ocean. This symbolizes that a state can only be strong when it rules the waves.[20]

Indonesia is an archipelago, and sea communications are therefore important for the economic viability of her territory. The coast washed by the Indian Ocean is generally surf-ridden with no good harbours except that of Tjilatjap in South Java. The opposite coast abounds in harbours and has very active sea traffic between the islands and externally. Indonesia's oil trade, the mainstay of her economy, is growing and her wealth of natural resources awaits large-scale exploitation. Indonesia is populated with a sea-faring people and has the potential to develop into a strong maritime power, if her resources can be properly harnessed and her economy well ordered.[21]

The growing super-power rivalry in the Indian Ocean was deplored by Indonesia, which highly values the tradition of an independent and active foreign policy. Accordingly, Indonesia supports the idea to have the Indian Ocean internationally declared as a Zone of Peace, free from foreign military power and bases.[22]

When the Cairo conference of the Non-aligned Nations condemned in October 1964, "the expressed intention of imperialist powers to establish bases in the Indian Ocean as a calculated attempt to intimidate the emerging countries of Asia and Africa and an unwarranted extension of the policy of neocolonialism and imperialism," Indonesia was the only nation which was a member of the non-aligned movement at that time from South East Asia[23].

Indonesia also supported the move which called upon all nations to "consider and respect the Indian Ocean as a Zone of Peace from which great power rivalries and competition as well as bases, conceived in the context of such rivalries and competition, either army, navy or airforce are excluded.[24]

At the UN General Assembly on 16 Dec. 1971, Indonesia endorsed Resolution 2832 (XXVI) entitled "Declaration of Indian Ocean as a Zone of Peace" and all subsequent resolutions confirming the resolution and urging the great powers to refrain from increasing their military presence in the Indian Ocean.

Indonesia was also placed on the *Ad hoc* Committee set up by the United Nations General Assembly in 1972, to take steps for the implementation of the UN resolution.

As early as March 1970 Adam Malik had stated that his country did not see any justification for foreign military bases in the Indian Ocean. He also regretted the "failure of super powers to understand the desire of many countries to make the Indian Ocean a Zone of Peace." He declared that if the USA enlarges its naval facilities on Diego Garcia, because the former Soviet Union possesses military facilities in the area, the Indian Ocean would become a "Zone of Confrontation instead of Peace." Thus he almost equated both the super powers as far as their naval activities in this area were concerned.[25]

While Indonesia has taken an interest in the developments in the Indian Ocean and has formally pledged its support to the concept of a Peace Zone, right from the beginning, it also finds the proposal rather "**unrealistic and impractical.**" According to Ali Moertopo, an Indonesian strategist, in the light of history and modern facts of power and vested interests, Indonesia is skeptical about its implementation. Any hope of neutralization of the Indian Ocean can only be seen as *'remote and idealistic'*.[26]

The Indonesian answer to secure peace, stability and security in the region is to maintain an equilibrium among the big powers i.e. "Reasonable balance at as low a level as possible" till the implementation of the UN resolution for the creation of a peace zone.

Indonesia's Indian Ocean Policy has undergone a significant change from a position of "**no presence**" (in the late sixties - support of defence cooperation among the Indian Ocean countries - Sri Lanka, India, Pakistan, Malaysia, Singapore and Indonesia, in order to defend the Indian Ocean) to a "**balanced presence**" (in the early Seventies - support of multinational presence through five powers - Britain, Malaysia, Singapore, Australia and New Zealand).[27]

However, Indonesia consistently supported the cause of creation of a Peace Zone in the Indian Ocean through all the international forums, which took up the issue. But when it found that the great powers do not pay any attention to the views of the littoral states and show no respect for the UN resolution or UN directives, it modified its stand. Now, it advocates balance in the great power presence at "**as low level as possible**" as an intermediate step while considering the **creation of a Peace Zone in the Indian Ocean as a long term and final solution of the problem.** With the changing times it has also started to increase its presence in the India Ocean partly to check the growing incidents of piracy and partly to protect its own national interests in the region.

Singapore

Strategically located in Southeast Asia and skirting a major international maritime route and the eastern gateway to the Indian Ocean, Singapore has immense geo-economic and geo-strategic importance.[28] Its focal position gives it an importance, out of all proportions, to its magnitude, however adjusted. It has both achieved greatness and greatness was thrust upon it by the eternal geography and the contemporary juncture of world politics.[29]

Singapore's strategy and foreign policy arise out of its strategic location and the interest of other powers in it besides its internal compulsions and its purposes.

Singapore's Indian Ocean Policy is decided by entirely different considerations. It has taken quite an independent stand on the Indian Ocean. Its geo-strategic location in the middle of Southeast Asia and between the Indian and Pacific Oceans plus its city state character are perhaps the main determinants of its Indian Ocean Policy.[30]

Singapore rejects the logic of the concept of a Zone of Peace in the Indian Ocean and facts that *"a pull out by the big powers does not automatically make it a Zone of Peace.*[31] As a result it abstained from voting on the historic resolution on the Indian Ocean in 1971.

It is also not against the presence of the non-littoral states in the Indian Ocean because "**it belongs to nobody and every body.**" It should be freely open to all nations.[32] It is happy to see all the foreign powers operating in the area, balancing each other.[33] Singapore did not or could not realize that the very idea of a balanced force appears very innocuous. It is fraught with several pitfalls and dangers for the Afro-Asian States. It undermines the very idea of converting the Indian Ocean Region into a Peace Zone. It gives the impression that the efforts of the Afro-Asian world towards that direction have totally failed and the only alternative left is to accept the state of affairs, and to legitimize the foreign presence in this area. Even if the scheme is accepted by the littoral states, which appears to be a remote possibility, there will still be several difficulties in its implementation.

Singapore's Indian Ocean Policy is a natural corollary of its leader's conviction that after three and a half decades of struggle for power to establish some kind of power balance in the Pacific Ocean, great powers will concentrate their attention on the Indian Ocean in the near future. In such a situation small nations are just helpless, having no voice. In the words of Singapore's Foreign Minister:

> "Any small nation which seeks to frustrate this grand design would be roughly brushed aside. If the question is whether it is the small nations or the super-powers who should inherit this derelict ocean, who should carve up positions of it, then the answer is (whether we like it or not), the Super Powers. The reason is that the Indian Ocean, now that the Super Powers have discovered the value of sea power, is too valuable strategically and commercially to be made a play thing of small nations diplomacy.[34] So the wise approach for the small nations would have been to take "the first step to make sure that the Indian Ocean is carved up between 'a few great powers' not only between the two Super Powers". He argued that, "We cease to be the masters of our fate and captains of our soul" because the successive steps would be the logical consequences of the first one".[35]

Southeast Asia as a region has been striving for neutralization and if this long term demand is achieved, Singapore can be an ideal base for the joint naval fleets of the ASEAN countries, as it is located nearly at the Centre of Southeast Asia and the troops and forces stationed there would have more ready and quick access to the likely trouble spots in the entire region, than from any other single location.

To achieve this the ASEAN states will have to loosen their ties with the external powers and build up a system of defence based on self-reliance and cooperation among the ASEAN states themselves. Throughout Southeast Asia, cooperation and conflict are not poles apart but co-exist within the same situation; which theme is dominant at a particular time can change very rapidly, not the least because South - East Asia is inescapably involved in world politics, strategy and economics and no impenetrably insulated regional cocoon can be created. In such a situation it can survive, cooperate and be useful to all.[36]

Malaysia

It has been the only country in Southeast Asia, which has extended unequivocal support to the Peace Zone proposal. It considers all foreign naval activity as a source of tension, having an adverse effect on the stability and security of the littoral states of the Indian Ocean.

Malaysia is a member of all important international forums, which have been advocating the creation of a Peace Zone in the Indian Ocean i.e. the NAM, Commonwealth of Nations and the United Nations, including the *Ad hoc* Committee set up by the General Assembly in 1972.

The creation of a Peace Zone in the Indian Ocean is to be treated as a pre-condition for the realization of the Malaysian dream of neutralization of Southeast Asia. Because, if outside powers remain in the Indian Ocean, making it a theatre of power-game then certainly the littoral countries would not be able to live in peace, unaffected by the happenings in the immediate strategic environment and South-East Asia is one of the most vulnerable areas for such influences.[37]

Burma/ Myanmar

Burma is the border between Southeast Asia and the Indian subcontinent. While its long coastline faces the Bay of Bengal and the Andaman Sea, high mountains separate it from China and India.[38]

Since its independence in 1948, it has adopted a policy of non-alignment attempting to exclude all foreign influences. Burma appears to have no extraordinary maritime ambitions and is happy to preserve her sovereignty in an atmosphere of peace.

Burma supports the Peace Zone concept and desires no external influence in her internal affairs.[39]

Australia

Up until the end of the 1960's Australia considered itself a country looking towards the Pacific. The necessity for Australia to change its orientation towards the Pacific and give the Indian Ocean proper attention came with the British announcement of withdrawing from the East of Suez which occurred at the same time as Western Australia was being developed economically with the result that Australia's Indian Ocean Coast (9,000 of the 12,000 miles Australian Coastline) and its ports gained in importance.[40] Of all the countries bordering the Indian Ocean, Australia can be compared in this respect only with India which has an equally strong interest in the Indian Ocean.

The two major political parties of Australia-Labour and Liberal-have entirely opposite perceptions of and policies towards the Indian Ocean Region. Whereas the Labour party identifies itself with Indian Ocean states and supports the Indian Ocean Peace Zone proposal, the Liberal party supports the United States naval build-up in the Indian Ocean.[41]

The Liberal party rejected the concept of the Indian Ocean Peace Zone but the Labour party stressed its solidarity with the aims of the Asian countries and the non-aligned movement and Australia became a member of the United Nations *ad hoc* committee considering the Indian Ocean Peace Zone proposal.

Thus we see that when the Liberal party comes to power it supports the US naval build-up in the Indian Ocean, and when the Labour Party is in power it tries to support the Indian Ocean Peace Zone proposal. Still, the overriding factor in deciding Australian policies towards the Indian Ocean is its security links with the United States, which have always been obligatory for Australia. Especially so since the British withdrawal from the East of Suez, leaving Australia without any other strong supporter in the Indian Ocean Region.

Australian support for the US naval presence in the Indian Ocean was directly linked to the British decision to withdraw from the area, specially because Australia perceives threat from communism in general and from the former Soviet and Chinese activities in the area in particular.

The Indian Ocean plays a vital role in Australian Security and prosperity and in spite of the differences between the two particular parties on essential tactics, there is a general agreement on the need to safeguard and further Australian interests in these waters.

Australia views the United States presence in Asia as an essential condition for its own security. So, despite the vast differences in the perceptions and policies of the two major political parties of the state, Australia cannot overlook its dependence on the United States resulting in close naval cooperation between the two countries-Australia being a continuous link in the overall US Indian Ocean strategy.

As a result Australia has always abstained from voting on the Indian Ocean Peace Zone proposal.

References

1. Mishra, K.P. "Quest for An International Order in the Indian Ocean", Allied, 1977, New Delhi, pp. 3-4.

2. Braun, Dieter, "The Indian Ocean; Region of Conflict or Peace Zone?" Oxford University Press, New Delhi, 1983, p. 20.
3. Mishra, K.P. *op. cit.* pp. 70-72.
4. Subramaniam, R.R.," South Africa's Strategic Significance in the Indian Ocean", Africa Quarterly,Vol.32, Nos. 1-4, 1992-93, pp. 171-72.
5. Anand, J.P. "Indian Ocean, Strategic Significance of Island Republic and Territories", IDSA Journal, Vol. XV, No.1, pp. 545-46.
6. Kohli, S.N. "Sea Power and the Indian Ocean, with Special Reference to India", Tata McGraw Hill, New Delhi, 1978, p. 136.
7. Chandra, S. "Iran's Role in the Indian Ocean" in T.T. Poulose (ed.) "Indian Ocean Power Rivalry", Young Asia, New Delhi, 74, pp. 103-104.
8. Kant, Ravi, "The Indian Ocean" A Strategic Posture for India" in T.T. Pulose, (ed.), *op. cit.*, p. 65.
9. Dowdy and Trood, (ed.) "The Indian Ocean: Perspectives on a Strategic Arena", p. 303.
10. Cottrell and Burell, "The Indian Ocean: Its Political Economic and Military Importance", Prager, USA, 1972, p. 237.
11. Sin, K.R. *op. cit.*, p. 181.
12. Kohli,S.N. *op. cit.*, p. 139.
13. Kohli, S.N., *op. cit*, p. 134
14. Pulose, T.T., (ed.) *op. cit.*, pp. 96-97.
15. *Ibid*, pp. 98-101.
16. Vali, *op. cit.*
17. Vali, *ibid*. pp. 106-107.
18. Moertopo, Maj. Gen. Ali, "Indonesia & The Indian Ocean," IDSA Journal, Vol. IX, No. 3, Jan-Mar. 1977, p. 214.
19. Kohli , S.N., "Sea Power and the Indian Ocean, with special reference to India", Tata McGraw Hill, New Delhi, 1978, p. 133.
20. Singh, Vishal, "Indonesia and the Indian Ocean", in T.T. Poulose (ed), *op. cit.*, p. 163.
21. Kohli, *op. cit.*, p. 134.
22. Moertopo, *op. cit.*, p. 214.
23. Pathak, Saroj, "India, South-East Asia and the Indian Ocean", IDSA, p. 90.

24. Moertopo, *op. cit.*, p. 215.
25. Singh, Vishal, *op. cit.*, p. 166.
26. Pathak, Saroj, *op. cit.*, p. 99.
27. Moertopo, *op. cit.*, p. 216.
28. Anand, J.P., "Indian Ocean: Strategic Significance Of Island Republics and Territories", IDSA Journal, Vol. XV, No. 1, July-Sept., 1982, p. 558-59.
29. Kakkar, A.N., "Singapore and Indian Ocean" in T.T. Poulsoe (ed.), *op. cit.*, pp. 144-45.
30. Pathak, Saroj, *op. cit.*, p. 102.
31. Sin, K.R., "The Indian Ocean: Big Powers and Local Response", Manohar, Delhi, 1977, p. 211.
32. Rajaratnam, "Singapore and Indian Ocean", in T.T. Poulose (ed.), *op. cit.*, p. 161.
33. Singh, K.R., *op. cit.*, p. 206.
34. Rajaratnam, *op. cit.*, p. 161.
35. Rajaratnam, *ibid*. p. 161.
36. Kakkar, in T.T. Poulose (ed.). *op. cit.*, p. 153.
37. Pathak, Saroj, *op. cit.*, p. 101.
38. Vali, *op. cit.*, p. 107.
39. Kohli, *op. cit.*, p. 134.
40. Braun, D., *op. cit.*, p. 115.
41. Bezboruah, Monoranjan, "US Strategy in the Indian Ocean: The International Response", Prager, USA, 1977, p. 200.

6

Role of IOR-ARC

The Indian Ocean has been for centuries a highway of commerce since the days of early civilizations. The Indian Ocean has been a centre for trade and people-to-people contact. This network of trade and other cultural links has always given it a distinct regional identity. Despite the diverse, cultural, religious dimensions and varied environment these countries are linked through the complex webs of history, politics, economics and their peculiar environment.

The 'Core' of 'the world' is in the Indian Ocean Region and all the countries excepting Australia and South Africa are in the United Nations' category of developing economies. The region's small countries like Seychelles and the larger ones like India and Australia, all have a stake in the preservation of peace and stability in the region and a shared interest in the rational exploitation of the ocean's immense potential.

The end of the cold war, South Africa's comeback to the international community and the opening of the economies of the region, particularly in South Asia, were a few factors that created a new political and economic environment for cooperation. "Changes in the global power-structure and sweeping structural reforms of international economic order facilitated regional dialogue across the Indian Ocean.[1] The development of an increasing number of regional blocs elsewhere in the world also urged the nations of this region to look for regional cooperation. This was a very important factor as regionalization does not come about unless the states in a particular region want it. It may come about through a more or less spontaneous or unintended convergence in terms of political regime and economic policy or security, but after one can identify a triggering political event which sets the process in motion. Nationally this political event is related to main players in the region, the policy makers, or regional great powers.

As far as the Indian Ocean Region is concerned a need had been pressing for an organized forum for regional cooperation mainly due to two factors:

First, the tempo of regionalism had been increasing rapidly, since the end of the cold war some new arrangements had emerged and the existing arrangements were growing stronger as regional interests sought and acquired fuller expression. Europe had the European Union (EU) and the Organization of Security and Cooperation in Europe (OSCE); Africa had the Organization of African unity (OAU) as well as the South Africa Development Community (SADC). The Asia-Pacific Region had Asia-Pacific Economic Cooperation (APEC), South East Asia had ASEAN and the ASEAN Regional Forum (ARF), and even South Asia had SAARC. only the Indian Ocean Region was without one such forum.

Second, with the formation of mega blocks in Europe, the Western Hemisphere and the Pacific Basin in the 1990's, the world economic environment had changed unfavourably for the countries of Afro-Asia, particularly so for those located in the low intensity trade areas. It was becoming well nigh impossible for them to improve their share in the balance of world trade. Until and unless they operated under the aegis of effective regional forums of their own, not only would they continue to lag behind the stronger and more aggressive regional forums of other regions, but the gap between the two might also have continued to widen. The vulnerable countries therefore had no option but to join or form effective regional trading blocks.[2]

Since then, in the changed world circumstances, attention is fast moving from geo-strategy and geo-politics to geo-economics. The emergence of regionalism and cooperation in Indian Ocean Region has increasingly been perceived as an effective tool in the new era of 'Economic Diplomacy'. The reasons are:

1. Regional cooperation has been increasingly seen as an instrument for ensuring peace, a goal important by itself, specially so given the present and potential tensons and conflicts in the area[3].
2. Since most states in the region are developing economies, regional cooperation is seen by them as an effective way of tackling the problems of economic development, particularly so for reducing their dependence on the industrialized North and for increasing their own bargaining power.
3. Regional cooperation is sought to be promoted in order to counterbalance protectionist and insular trends witnessed in recent years in may parts of the Northern Hemisphere, and
4. Regional cooperation is seen as a way of promoting a polycentric world economy as against one that is entirely dominated by the United States of America.[4]

The need to reshape international relations following the collapse of the erstwhile Soviet Union was particularly pressing in the Indian Ocean Region. Many of the states in the region had attempted to steer a middle path between the great powers during the cold war, even if the economies of the majority of the less economically developed countries tended to be based on the interpretations of socialism. By the early 1990's these economies were in crises. The same was true in the post apartheid South Africa, which was seeking a total reconstruction of the discriminatory capitalist economy of the apartheid era. In Australia, too, by the last decade of the century there was a concerted and steady move in the direction of economic deregulation and the pursuit of a new regionally based place in the world.[5]

Spread over three main continents, viz. Africa, Asia and Australia and essentially of a maritime and economically diverse nature, the Indian Ocean Region is an interesting model of intra-regional economic cooperation. The region has passed through several phases in the post World War II period. Viewed first as a **'zone of cold war rivalries and conflicts'** it was later on projected as a potential **'zone of peace'** and now it is beginning to explore itself as a **'zone of co-operation'**.

How it came about? The Background

The genesis for creating a regional forum of the Indian Ocean Rim countries can be traced as far back as to the Afro-Asian conference at Bandung. Later on Sri-Lanka and Tanzania had proposed the Indian Ocean Zone of Peace (IOZP) concept. Such proposals had however lacked the consensus on the basic objectives despite the non-aligned states adopting a declaration at Lusaka in 1970 calling upon all states to exclude great power rivalries and competition from this region. The India Ocean Commission (IOC) was formed in 1982 by the island nations of Mauritius, Madagascar, Seychelles, Comoros and Reunion for fostering economic development through regional cooperation, but had failed to broaden the oceanic agenda. The Indian Ocean Marine Affairs Cooperation Council (IOMAC) was initiated in 1955 to provide a framework for dealing with marine resources science and environmental issues but this also could not get the required momentum. Then came another effort to bring the countries together which was based on both track I and II methods.

Track One Conference - Port Louis- March 1995

The South African president Nelson Mandela started it all during his state visit to New Delhi in January 1995, when he declared that,

"The natural urge of the facts of history and geography that Nehru spoke of should broaden itself to include exploring the concept of an Indian Ocean Rim for socio-economic cooperation and to improve the lot of the developing nations in multilateral institutions such as the United Nations, Commonwealth and Non-Aligned Movement".

As a result an intergovernmental (first-track) conference was held in Port Louis (Mauritius) from 29-31 March 1995. Seven Indian Ocean Rim countries that came to be known as M-7 or sponsors of (IOR-ARC)- South Africa, Australia, India, Mauritius, Kenya, Singapore and Oman attended this conference.

In the spirit of transparent regionalism, it was agreed to promote sustained and balanced growth of the peoples of the participating countries with clear linkages to human resource and trading. The guiding principles adopted at the conference were:

1. Cooperation should be based on the respect for sovereign equality, territorial integrity, political independence, mutual benefit and peaceful co-existence.
2. Such cooperation should not be a substitute for bilateral and multilateral cooperation but should reinforce and complement such forums of cooperation.
3. All sovereign states of the Indian Ocean region will be eligible for membership, but expansion beyond the initial seven participants should be necessarily consensus-based.
4. Bilateral and other issues, likely to generate controversy and be an impediment to regional cooperative efforts, shall be excluded from the deliberations.[6]

This track one conference paved the way for track two efforts, which culminated in the establishment of IOR-ARC in 1997.

Track Two Conference - Perth June 1995

Australia initiated a 'second track' conference for exploring the scope of regional cooperation at Perth from 11-13 June. 23 countries were invited to join this conference and 123 participants (in their personal capacities) attended it. A distinct feature of this meeting was that it discussed the aspect of the global and regional security arrangements in general and the security characteristics of the Indian Ocean Region in particular, and the non-military security issues for their trans-boundry and international impact and the need for a multinational and regional cooperation.

The 'Economic Working Group' identified two broad agendas. The first on business facilitation such as, taxes, currency convertibility, trade promotion and a regional business directory. **The second** encompassed technology transfers, transport, telecommunications and human resource development.

'The Other Issues Working Group' discussed subjects like education, health, law and justice, sports, environmental issues, drugs, terrorism, maritime cooperation, economic opportunities and comprehensive security approaches including their applicability to maritime resource protection, defence cooperation, non-proliferation, the security of small island-states, safety at sea, anti-piracy, UN peace keeping and preventive diplomacy. In a way this spilled over into security related issues which had been meticulously kept out at the Mauritius meeting so as not to divert the Indian Ocean Rim countries from effective regional economic co-operation.

Later a number of 'formal' and 'informal' meetings at different places led the way to convert the ideas of cooperation into reality. But before any formal initiative could be launched, many issues had to be discussed and agreed upon, such as;

1. **Geographical Coverage-** Although the question of hinterland was advocated (South Africa), it was broadly agreed that countries having direct outlet to the Indian ocean basin would only be invited to join the association. In this way more than 40 countries from South and South East Asia, West Asia, Africa and Oceania (Australia and New Zealand) were identified as members of the grouping. This decision thus excluded the Persian Gulf and the Red sea and disabled some important and influential coastal states like Saudi Arabia from admission and marginalized the land-locked states whose transit is oriented to the Indian ocean.

2. **Economic Grouping in a Heterogeneous Region-** Another important issue was how to establish economic cooperation in a region, which had immense diversities of ethnicity, culture and religion. Not only this, the countries also differed in their size, levels of development, degree of openness and political structures /ideologies.

   These differences were so vast that some scholars argued in favour of various circles within the group/association that could move with different speeds. The left Arc of the Indian Ocean Rim (Mainly SAARC, West Asia and Africa) could go on one speed and the right Arc of the ocean (ASEAN and Oceania) on a different speed. In addition there could also be smaller rings of bilateral and sub-regional blocks with their own arrangements and speeds.[7]

3. **Membership of Other Trading Blocks-** Almost all the members are also members of one trading block or another. So some kind of coordination mechanism with the existing trading and economic blocs and needs has to be worked out. South Africa is more interested in the South Atlantic and Australia in the Pacific. In such a situation complete commitment to IOR-ARC would be difficult to achieve.

4. **Political issues-** It is true that political issues are kept out of its agenda but sooner or later questions regarding peace and security in the ocean are sure to crop up, specially regarding maritime security. The differences in such issues among the member states are not unknown to anybody. To keep such issues out of its agenda would be difficult and if they creep in directly or indirectly, it would be the end of the association.

5. **Influential Members-** India, South Africa and Australia are the three influential states of this region and their role and influence is to be taken into account in any discussions regarding the region. These states are the only ones that possess all necessary attributes (political, economic, cultural and even military) to effectively exercise a certain

leadership at the regional scale. All three play the card of South-South relations and try to gain something out of the emergent regionalism. India pursuing its old ambition of regional pre-eminence (with an eventual international recognition that could, for example, take the form of a permanent membership at the UN Security Council), Australia looking mostly to seize good economic opportunities that arise from developing economies (e.g. the Mozal project in Mozambique) and emergent markets (e.g. the United Arab Emirates), and South Africa extending its interests and influence far over its traditional privileged area covering Southern Africa and the South-West Indian Ocean Islands.

Whatever the economic objectives of the IOR-ARC, ultimately the cooperation will have to extend to peace and security; otherwise the ideal emancipation of the Indian Ocean Rim as an Indian oceanic community that effectively controls the region will never fully be realized. And as earlier maintained, this is a very tricky issue that will have to be dealt with very carefully keeping national sensitivities in consideration of all at all the times. The importance of such considerations and cooperation is evident from the early response to the Declaration of thc Indian Ocean as a Zone of Peace. Initially a shared regional interest (even during the cold war era) had very effectively and formally bonded the states of the region together. Whatever the reasons for the failure of the IOPZ academic works, the diplomatic negotiations and political debates that have been achieved in relation to it have promoted the concept of the Indian ocean community and have also helped us come so far in this direction.

Despite all these challenges and problems a certain degree of complementarity in trade structures and the geo-political situation of these countries convinced the states that they could benefit if they were together. So after two years of discussions, deliberations and meetings at various levels IOR-ARC came into being in 1997.

Establishment of IOR-ARC

Three different solidarities can be explained as the root of this organization.

1. **The promotion of South-South relations** and common interests which are developed in reaction to both the colonial past and the actual economic domination of the North, and thus it implies an emancipation from the influences of the large foreign powers.

2. **The Indian diaspora**, which represents a significant Indian Oceanic factor that has already developed commercial, financial and cultural networks covering the whole region and acts at the same time as a very effective means of diffusion for India's influence.

3. **Islam,** which is the most common religion and specially in a crescent that goes from the Comoros Islands to Malaysia and Indonesia, covers the Middle East with a cultural factor that could eventually weigh a lot in countering India's regional pre-eminence.

If these three regional solidarities are far more than only potential factors, they are also limited by the fact that none of them is neither specific to the region nor of first/prime significance in the whole region. The admission of France for Reunion and Mayotte will probably not change the general situation in regard to these solidarities, but if the Red Sea and the Persian Gulf coastal states (especially Egypt and Saudi Arabia) were to be more closely bound to the Indian Oceanic Regionalism and gain IOR-ARC membership as well as Pakistan, then Indian and Muslim influences could find a fertile ground for competition, if not confrontation, in addition to the desired cooperation. At the same time, leaving those states out of the regionalization process will mean that big regional players will be left aside, and therefore the strength of the regional association would diminish. Thus, considering the main solidarities on which the regionalism will evolve, ideological and political issues also become significant even if economy remains the official and declared objective of the IOR-ARC.[8]

The first meeting of the working group of M-7 which was set up to outline the principles and objectives, the scope of activities and work programme was held in Port Louis in August 1995. The working group decided on the first expansion by doubling to include seven more countries (N-7). Indonesia, Madagascar, Malaysia, Mozambique, Sri Lanka, Tanzania and Yemen, which were invited to join the next inter-governmental meeting (IGM). India was mandated to coordinate the preparation of a charter for the IOR grouping. Mauritius was assigned the task of coordinating the work programme. The second working group meeting was held in Port Louis in May 1996. The meeting agreed on the draft text of the charter as well as a draft work programme.

The third working group meeting involving the M-7 was held in September 1996 back to back with the second Inter-Governmental Meeting (IGM) of all fourteen members. The IGM recommended the charter for formal adoption at the first ministerial meeting. A work programme of ten specific projects was adopted for immediate implementation.

These projects rclated to

1. Cooperation in standards and accredition.
2. Indian Ocean Rim business centre and IORNET.
3. Investment facilitation and promotion.
4. IOR chair in Indian Ocean Studies and Associate Fellows.
5. Trade promotion programme and IOR trade fair in 1997.
6. Development, upgrading and management of seaports, maritime transport, insurance and reinsurance.
7. Human Resource Development.
8. Working towards complementarity- Comparative analysis of existing multilateral and regional economic and trade policy arrangements and processes.
9. Tourism promotion and development, and
10. Technology advancement in the Indian ocean region.[10]

The second IGM marked the IOR-ARC's attainment of critical mass for constructively moving this initiative forward. The IGM of 14 members agreed to a draft charter for formal adoption by the meeting of the foreign ministers of IOR-ARC convened in Mauritius from March 5-7, 1997. The ministerial meeting thus marked the formal official launching of IOR-ARC.

In his keynote address at the launching of the IOR-ARC, the Prime Minister of Mauritius, Navinchandra Ramgoolam, set out its objectives clearly. He said, "Our association will not be driven by the forces of fear or insularity, or by a strategic desire to merge the individual identity or political sovereignty of its members into some greater whole, but by the voluntary and enthusiastic spirit of their disparate governments and people for mutual support in the great struggle for material progress". He also declared that "Respect for and preservation of the distinctive hallmarks of our separate identities and our freedom of action and creation of a common ground would be a prime concern. The charter, modest and flexible as it is," he further said, "is not meant to be a grand prescription for a closed and protective club of nations seeking the economic power to entrench themselves against the currents and trends sweeping the world. It is a free and open association of sovereign nations.[11]

Since 1997 the membership of the association has increased. At the council of ministers of the IOR-ARC at Muscat in January 2000, five new members were admitted. The People's Republic of Bangladesh, The Islamic Republic of Iran, The Republic of Seychelles, The Kingdom of Thailand and The United Arab Emirates. Five dialogue partners have also been identified; The Peoples Republic of China, The Arab Republic of Egypt, The Republic of France, Japan and The United Kingdom. The Indian Ocean Tourist Organization (IOTO) has been given the status of an observer. Thus the organization has created the critical mass necessary for it to take up the challenges brought about by globalization and the internationalization of economies, and is increasingly being recognized on the international level.

The IOR-ARC has at present more or less completed the first phase of bringing its peoples together in a spirit of friendship and solidarity. There is definitely a sense of belonging as well as collective security, Now it has come to a critical juncture to move the cooperation process forward at a faster speed-to address the work programmes, to complete feasibility studies and to implement the projects. There is a wide portfolio of projects undertaken by the Academic Group, the Business Forum and the Working Group on Trade and Investment.

Problems in the way of cooperation: Initially the flush of enthusiasm had kept the IOR-ARC going but as the time passed IOR-ARC had to face many problems that can be divided into two categories, internal and external.

Internally the basic problem was that there was no clear direction concerning either the functions of or relationship with one another of the three basic groups, business, academic and official. As a result within a couple of years the governance of the organization had in effect become the prerogative of the official group with the academic and business groups exercising minimum influence. By the year 2000, the academic and business components of this tripartite system were all but moribund apart from some officially sponsored and irregular input.

Externally, the world was facing unexpected events that undermined interest in the organization. Strong bilateral links could have provided a strong foundation for the IOR-ARC. All but the 14 countries that had signed the charter had little or no direct contact with one another in the international area before IOR-ARC had come into being.

The East Asian economic crisis of 1997 also distracted Southeast Asian members from the IOR-ARC, as now the focus was shifting from multilateralism to bilateralism. Such a development received further encouragement as the world economy hovered on the brink of recession and individual states moved to secure their economies. In Southeast Asia individual states in part turned from ASEAN in search of bilateral free trade agreements elsewhere, and across the Indian Ocean Region there was a great rush to establish free trade agreements with major extra-regional economies not, let it be noted with one another, except for Australia and Singapore. By the end of the 1990's there was a clear decline in interest in IOR-ARC on the part of its three major supporters-Australia, India and South Africa-though all three had their own different reasons.

As a result though the membership of the association increased, even Japan and France showed an interest in becoming its member, but serious commitment to the organization declined.[12]

Suggestions: Still it is not too late. The Association could be revived and revitalized if sincere efforts to do so are made, e.g.

1. The basis of cooperation has to be widened. Trade and investment are vital issues but other issues like comprehensive and maritime security are also important and can be included in the agenda.
2. Regional governments will have to commit enough resources to keep the organization going. Similarly business and academic groups will have to be made more active.
3. Instead of concentrating on rapid growth the need is to consolidate past gains on a priority basis. For this members will have to move forward in a cautious and evolutionary manner.
4. A collective action to prevent the over exploitation of the ocean's resources and over-pollution can bring the member nations together immediately as all are concerned by these problems instead of economy, polity or security. Human security is another area, which can make member states come closer without any doubts. Moreover India's 'Look East Policy' and Australia and South Africa's "Look West Policy' still can give favourable results and save the organization from plummeting into the darkness for ever.

India and IOR-ARC

India's foreign policy has had one cherished aim: to bring the Afro-Asian nations together. The non-aligned movement had brought them together politically and IOR-ARC fulfilled the need of economic cooperation. So, it was natural for India to give its all-out support to the IOR-ARC.

Speaking at the first meeting of the Indian Ocean Rim countries in March 1995, the leader of the Indian delegation Mr. V.K. Grover remarked, "We are today embarking on a difficult exercise to give concrete shape and form to what has so far been a spontaneous interlocking of the littoral communities of the Indian Ocean Region. Our civilizational interactions and shared experiences bind us. Also, the Indian Ocean has traditionally been, and continues to be, a vital highway, source of food and raw materials, and a centre of commercial and maritime activities. Its potentiality is without limit if we guide and exploit it jointly. These are reasons enough that we should now attempt a mere structured and synergetic coming together. History lies in the past but also before us to make the **Indian Ocean based regional economic cooperation which is an idea whose time has come**[13] When the IOR-ARC was formally set up on March 6, 1997, it was aptly described by the then external affairs minister of India, I.K. Gujaral as the 'Recovery of History" and "Vital Reaffirmation " of the vision of Afro-Asian partnership. India's interests in the IOR-ARC are manifold such as:

1. Ocean based regional cooperation has become important over the years and all the major countries of the world were busy trying to reorient their economic policies in this direction. Since India has a vast coastline, large EEZ and vital stakes, economic and strategic in the ocean it also realized the importance of sea-borders though a little to late. So India also tried to protect its national interests through the IOR-ARC.

2. In the fast changing world scenario most of the Afro-Asian countries too had adopted policies of economic liberalization and India too wanted markets for its exports

and hoped to find the same in the member countries of the IOR-ARC.

3. India also hopes to further its claim on a permanent seat in the United Nations Security Council through consolidating its economic status.

4. Due to its geo-strategic location India cannot afford to ignore any developments in the Indian Ocean without jeopardising its own national interests. This becomes much more important in view of the emerging non-traditional maritime threats to the peace and security in the region like sea-piracy and terrorism.

5. Human security and marine environment are two other issues that are vital for India. Looking at the dangers to human security, which became evident by the Tsunami-on 26 December 2004 the need to cooperate has become vital. Similarly protection of the living and non-living maritime resources together with the marine environment is vital due to their complex bio-spherical relationship.

All these interests, to name only a few, will keep India interested in developments in the Indian Ocean and hence IOR-ARC as well.

REFERENCES

1. For details please see, McPherson, Kenneth, "Indian Ocean Regional Dialogues: An Australian Perspective", in India-Australia Public Policy Conference, Indian Ocean Centre, Perth and Centre for Policy Research, New Delhi. 1996.
2. Mehta, Rajesh, "Indian Ocean Rim; Economic and Trade Issues", Strategic Analysis, Vol. XX (2), May 1997, pp. 243-262.
3. Murthy, Gautam, "The Indian Ocean Rim Initiative", Journal of Indian Ocean Studies, Vol. 3. No. 2, March, 1996, pp. 156-166.
4. Saeed, Amera, "An Economic Forum for The Indian Ocean Region". Regional Studies (Islambad). Vol XIV (I) Winter, 1995-96, pp. 59-95.
5. McPherson, Kenneth, "Indian Ocean Regional Dialogues". *op. cit.*

6. Roy, Mihir, "Indian Ocean Trading Blocks- Cure for Afro-Asian Seablindness", Journal of Indian Ocean Studies, Vol. 2, No.3, July 1995, pp. 223-229.
7. See, Sachdeva, Gulshan, "IOR-ARC at Crossroads", Paper presented at the Indian Ocean Research Group (IORG) Inaugural Conference, Chandigarh, 18-22 November 2002.
8. Bouchard, Christian," Geographical Setting of Indian Ocean Region", Journal of Indian Ocean Studies, vol.11, No.2. August, 2003, pp.214-233.
9. "India in IOR-ARC", World Focus, 208, April, 1997, pp. 11-15.
10. Chhabra, Hari Mohan," Economic Cooperation in Indian Ocean Rim" World Focus, *Ibid*., pp. 3-4.
11. Chackravarty, Nitish "Ambitious Association", World focus, *ibid*., pp. 7-8.
12. McPherson, IORG conference, *op. cit.*
13. Grover, V.K. "India and the Indian Ocean Rim Community" Journal of Indian Ocean Studies, Vol. I, No. 3, June 1995, pp. 219-222.

7

Regional and extra-regional navies in the Indian Ocean

The Indian Ocean region holds fifty per cent of the off-shore oil reserves, sixty five per cent of the strategic raw minerals like Uranium, thirty one per cent gas, comprises thirty per cent of the total world population, is a potentially large consumer market and has strong economies to match consumerism. All these factors make the region attractive for the regional and extra regional powers; hence we witness the ever increasing presence of various navies in this region of turmoil. The interests and stakes of the regional and extra-regional powers in this volatile region can be summed up in the following manner:

Interests of extra-regional and regional power in the region.

1. Access to the resources and potential markets of the region is the great motivating factor behind the increasing presence of the regional as well as the extra-regional powers in this region.

2. To exploit and benefit from the riches of this region the trade routes from and to this region have to be kept open in all situations. The Indian Ocean provides the shortest and most economical trade routes (Sea Lines of Communication). On these very routes are situated the most difficult **'choke points'** which pose the problem of keeping them open specially in view of non-traditional threats to maritime security like piracy and terrorism to their surrounding areas.

3. The region gains in importance due to its proximity to Antarctica.
4. What makes the presence of extra-regional powers strong in the region is the fact that the littoral states so far have not been successful in making their presence felt on these waters. Their failure in putting up a strong joint front/ organization provides ample scope for the extra-regional navies to operate with unrestricted flexibility in the ocean and look for and establish new island bases in addition to maintaining and strengthening the current ones.

The regional / littoral countries of the region have also awakened to the importance of their surrounding waters, though a little late, and now are trying to protect and promote their interests in the region. These specific interests of the countries of the region are:

1. Their national security which largely depends on the protection of their sea frontiers.
2. Maintenance of their freedom of shipping on which depends their international trade, and
3. Protection of their maritime resources, both living and non-living, which are growing in importance by the day.

Though many countries are accepted as countries of the Indian Ocean Region and many more put forward their claims to be recognized and accepted as one on the basis of their use of the ocean, due to limits of this study only a few of them are studied in this chapters i.e.

1. India
2. Pakistan
3. Sri Lanka
4. South Africa
5. Australia
6. Japan
7. France
8. China

As mentioned earlier in this work, the focus of strategists has shifted from the Atlantic-Pacific to the Pacific-Indian Ocean[1] due to economic as well as strategic reasons. Two main reasons make The Indian Ocean Region susceptible to outside influence: one political instability in the region coupled with arms and nuclear-arms race among the countries of the region and, two, the underdeveloped economies of most of the countries of the region and lack of resources and technologies to protect their maritime resources.

The situation becomes worse due to mutual hostilities in the region that has not helped the establishment of an effective regional organization for regional cooperation. Growing tensions in this region are very likely to provide an opportunity for foreign military forces to intervene, either directly or indirectly, under the banner of the Untied Nations. The Indian Ocean states will do well to take note of recent developments both in various international fora and legal regimes concerning high seas, territorial waters, continental shelves and Exclusive Economic Zones and proposed amendments to them to protect their own national interests.

To consolidate their presence in the region the extra-regional powers that have high stakes in the region have been trying to maintain, strengthen and acquire new bases in this region. History is a witness to the fact that, more often than not military deployments are preceded by naval deployment for power projection and deterrence. The large scale extra - regional presence in the Gulf and the recent Chinese initiatives in the Indian Ocean can be taken as a few indications of the trends for the future.

Changing Role of Navies: Traditionally the role of the navy could be classified into four broad categories:

1. Policing,
2. Diplomatic,
3. Crisis Management, and
4. Military.

With the changes in the political and geo-strategic environment, some of these roles have become predominant. The end of the cold war and the consequent changes in world political equations have brought about these changes. The policing role entails the protection of the resources, enforcing national maritime laws relating to merchant shipping, fiscal, fishing, marine environment, contraband control, drug running and immigration.

As far as the diplomatic role of the navies is concerned, they can create a favourable national image abroad. A warship can be a symbol of goodwill as well as a threat or can be used to intimidate the adversary by its sheer presence 'over there'.

The concept of freedom of the seas makes the navies a potent instrument in handling crisis. In the changed global order it has become imperative for the navies to establish and strengthen coordination procedures to be effective in any crisis situation, especially with diplomatic services, merchant navy and other ocean agencies.

With the changing world scenario non-traditional maritime threats like piracy, terrorism, illegal human traffic, drug running, environmental hazards, human security, etc, have expanded the role of the navies. As a result the nations of this region also have awakened to their security on the water fronts. They are now trying to make their navies blue water navies (e.g., China and India) and to modernise them keeping in view the changed and enhanced role they are expected to play.

India

Sub-continental India has a coastline of 6300 kilometres, with the island territories of Lakshadweep and Andaman and the Nicobar islands adding another 1200 kilometres. This coastline harbours eleven major, twenty intermediate and one hundred and forty-four minor ports. When the new law of the sea are applied to the country coastline, it gives India a staggering 2.2 million square kilometres of Exclusive Economic Zone (EEZ).

India's natural outlet is towards the sea through which ninety five per cent of its overseas trade passes. The country's sea-lanes are economically important and serve as vital sea - borne trade routes through the Indian Ocean. India's other maritime interests include high value assets in the form of off-shore oil and the vast potential of minerals and sea bed resources in the water surrounding it. In addition India has immense fishing interests in its EEZ, and the local shipbuilding industry has seen a resurgence in recent years largely due to India's urge of self-reliance.

The growth of the Indian navy has mainly been commensurate with the country's expanding maritime interests and should be seen in that light only. Here, it is also to be remembered that the maritime interests of a country primarily concern its security and economy and have a natural tendency to expand with time and this very thing has happened in the case of India.

As has been mentioned in the earlier chapters, India didn't pay adequate attention to its naval defence despite the suitable and timely warnings issued by scholars like K.M. Pannikar and Gen. K.B. Vaidya. Even though India was a naval power in the ancient times, since independence it concentrated only on its land frontier due to a variety of reasons. As a result the naval defence of India got neglected. Due to the strategic myopia and dwindling budgetary support India's naval capabilities and force levels got stagnated. All this happened despite the history teaching its policy makers two important lessons:

Firstly, the neglect of maritime power can culminate in a cessation of sovereignty, and secondly, it takes decades to revert to being a considerable maritime power after a period of neglect and decline.

Despite the ample warnings and cautions India failed to pay enough attention to its naval defence for a long time. It was the Indo-Pakistan war of 1971 which was fought over the issue of independence of the then East-Pakistan (now

Bangladesh) followed by the Oil crisis of 1973 that India too, like many others, began to realize the importance of its surrounding waters. Since then, the Indian navy has come a long way, slowly but gradually.

Initially the Indian Navy had inherited a very modest collection of five frigates and six mine sweepers. As compared to that modest beginning the Indian navy of today comprises of a three dimensional combat force which is capable of performing multifarious tasks. The teeth of the navy are the ships, submarines and aircraft of its Western and Eastern fleets. The elements of the fleet include aircraft carriers, versatile missile destroyers, indigenous missile frigates and missile corvettes. The amphibious ships provide the navy with a ship lift capability. India operates a 130 ship navy with 46000 uniformed and 48000 civilian personnel. Most recent acquisitions include Admiral Gorshkov, the formation of Far Eastern Naval Command and the launch of the latest naval port INS Kadamb (part of project Seabird) in the state of Karnataka. India also held its first ever International Fleet Review in February 2001.

The classic constitutes of sea power have remained unchanged in the last century - naval power, technology, port and maritime infrastructure. Political will, sea-faring population and economic strength have also only gained significance over the years, instead of losing it.

Admiral Madhvendra Singh termed the decade of 1985-1995 as a 'lost decade' which aptly sums up the attention paid to the Indian navy during that time. During this 'lost decade' the navy had bought next to nothing from abroad and had not even ordered anything substantial from its own shipyards. No orders were placed for surface combatants or submarines except only three warships. This happened when all other navies, to name just a few, Chinese, French and Japanese in addition to those of South East Asian nations, were trying to register their presence in this region where the destiny of the world is to be decided. Admiral Madhvendra Singh is also largely quoted as saying on the state of affairs in the Indian

Navy during the lost decade, "One pays for this two decades later, so we have to order more and extend the life of the ships in the service."

It may be said that largely due to the Admiral's efforts and of the people like him, and helped by international circumstances the government of India at last woke up to the need of the hour and started paying attention to the requirements of the Indian navy. As a result of this renewed interest in the defence of India's naval frontiers, the current decade can be called the 'navy's decade'. Now India has started reviving its naval defence and is aiming to make its navy 'a blue water navy' to project its national interests.

This change in perception has also been helped by the events of post 9/11 world situation and the 'Iraq War', which made very explicit the vital role a navy can play in modern warfare. The changed perception of the government is reflected in its budget allocations of specially two years i.e. in the year 2001-2002 the defence budget was given a hike of 13.8% to work out the details of FENC and in the year 2003-2004 a hike of 200% was given to acquire the Gorshkov and other new ships. India has also stepped up its naval cooperation with the regional as well as extra-regional powers. Over the past decade it has held a series of joint-naval exercises with countries like the United States of America, France, China and Japan, and nearer home it has been holding annual naval exercises code named 'Milan' with its south-east Asian neighbours to enhance naval cooperation and fight terrorism / piracy by effectively patrolling the international waters. Here it would be appropriate to look into the establishment of FENC, International Fleet Review and establishment of INS Kadamb to trace the major steps of development of the Indian Navy in recent times.

Far Eastern Naval Command (FENC)

To take better care of the country's exclusive economic zone in both the Bay of Bengal and the Indian Ocean, to monitor, control and prevent piracy in the vital sea lanes of the Straits of Malacca and for better surveillance and intelligence to keep a watch on any hostile activities, FENC was first proposed in 1995. The new command was proposed to be established at Port Blair off the Andaman and Nicobar island coast. To help establish this command, on which the work started later than originally expected, a 13.8% hike in the defence budget for the year 2001-2002 was given.

The establishment of this command was part of India's defence diplomacy to monitor and control piracy. It was expected to cost Rs. 10,000 crores and was to be partially funded by the USA (Clinton Administration had earlier given Rs. 50 crores to Bangladesh just to facilitate its war-ships anchor at Chittagong). This shows how much importance the US administration was placing upon its presence in the IOR. The USA has vital stakes in the region and it required a base in the East since it has lost the Subic Bay naval base in the Philippines and has also to quit Okinawa base in Japan. Hence, its interest in the new command established by India.

India, in addition to other reasons, was concerned due to increasing Chinese presence and activities in the region including the South China Sea. The issue of special concern was the establishment of a naval base, helped by China, on the Cocoas Islands (Myanmar) just 45 kilometres away from the Southern tip of the Great Nicobar Islands in 1995. This base could very conveniently be used by the Chinese to the detriment of India's national interests. India's fears were not without reason too; they are justified looking at the past activities of China in the past and in the plans it has for future in the IOR.

International Fleet Review[2]

Independent India held its first ever International Fleet Review from 15-20 February 2001 to commemorate fifty years of India as a republic. Its aim was to enhance military to military exchanges with navies from friendly countries and to foster a spirit of friendship and cooperation, essential to be successful on the high seas. Theme of this IFR was 'Bridges of Friendship' which was amply emphasized during the whole exercise. Earlier India had Fleet reviews by the Supreme Commander of its armed forces in the years, 1953, 1964, 1966 (When INS Vikrant made its appearance), 1969 (the submarine arm of the navy made its debut) 1976 and 1989. This international fleet review was successful in its aim and attracted the presence of all friendly countries to the prestigious ceremony.

Admiral Gorshkov[3]

On 20 January 2004, India finally signed the deal to acquire the 44,900 ton Russian aircraft carrier, Admiral Gorshkov. Named after Admiral Sergei Gorshkov, the father of the Soviet Unions blue water navy, it is to replace INS Vikrant, India's first aircraft carrier that had been commissioned in 1961. Admiral Gorshkov which comes to India as a free gift was retired by the Russian navy in 1994, after budget - cuts made operations unsustainable. Before it can become operational it will have to be refurbished. It has been lying alongside in Severodvinsk in the White Sea near Arkhangelsk since 1996. Though India only has to bear the cost of upgradation for the Gorshkov it is still estimated at a staggering Rs. 30 billion and the modifications are expected to take almost three years to be complete. Though admiral Gorshkov comes to India despite vehement criticism from the former Chief of Naval Staff Admiral J.G. Nadkarni on various counts[4] and after close to a decade's deliberations the operationalization of Gorshkov will be a tricky question. But, this may lead to improved inter-services cooperation which is necessary for India's defence forces.

INS Kadamb

INS Kadamb, India's largest naval base, exclusively for the use of the navy was commissioned on 31st May 2005, in the state of Karnataka.

The first phase of project seabird, the naval base, arguably, Asia's most advanced and the country's first with a ship lift facility cost about Rs. 1,026 crores and can accommodate 11 ships including an aircraft carrier.

This project was started in 2000 and has three phases in all that are expected to be completed at the total cost of Rs 1825 crores. With the commissioning of INS Kadamb only first phase of this project has been completed. Inaugurating the base India's defence minister Mr. Pranab Mukherjee said", with the commissionig of this naval base the navy will fulfil the responsibility of defending the country and safeguarding the exclusive economic zone.

INS Kadamb developed at Karwar, a natural harbour in Karnataka, is to house some of the Navy's most potent weapons destroyers, stealth frigates and possibly even the soon-to-be acquired Scorpene sub-marines, this important step towards modernizing the defence forces has also kept human security in view. A sum of Rs. 156 crores has been spent for the rehabilitation of all those people who had to be displaced due to the construction of this base.[6]

These new acquisitions by the Indian Navy may help India's policy planners to help achieve the much required, "Shift from power at sea" to power from the sea but it also requires India to behave and appear to be behaving in a much more responsible manner. Like other countries India has a three fold interest in the Indian Ocean, maritime, resource-based and strategic. But as a regional power and as the largest country in the region, India has to be more conscientious about respecting the rights of her smaller neighbours and be responsive to their interests. India has to bear the onus of greater maturity, sophistication and responsible behaviour[7] to develop Confidence-Building Measures (CBM's), in the region and help develop a distinct Indian Ocean Community.

These sentiments are also echoed in Geoffrey Tills words who, quoting from Sir Julian Corbett (considered equivalent to American Alfred Thayer Mahan), has written, "maritime power needs to be exercised with restraint lest it prove counter productive."[8] He had recommended that Britain strive to be seen as sensitive, modest, pragmatic and restrained. Britain should concentrate on limited, cost effective aims of keeping the system going, trading with advantage, on making money and being secure. These words hold true for modern-day India too as being the biggest kid on the maritime scene in the Indian Ocean.

Pakistan

Since its creation in 1947 the Pakistan Navy (PN) had to grapple with myriad problems ranging from limited funds, few naval platform it received at the time of partition under the 'Armed Forces Reconstitution Committee (AFNC) recommendation to lack of awareness among policy makers about the vital role of the navy in national defence. The navy could not find itself a logical place in national defence despite the fact that it was the only means of safeguarding Pakistan's eastern flank some 2600 nautical miles away. The continental mind-set in Pakistan was so strong that the navy was considered insignificant in the country' defence strategy. Consequently, the navy did not find favour with the ruling elite and its budgetary allocations remained low.[9] The navy was only expected to keep the sea lanes of communication open. In the event of a major war the navy in cooperation with friendly nations was to ensure unrestricted use of the sea lanes and during the limited war it was to carry out the task all by itself.

The potential threat to Pakistan Navy was seen as originating from the Indian Navy. Still, the Indian Ocean posed no great worry to Rawalpindi until well after the end of the Ayub Era. The story began to change only after the emergence of Bangladesh when the lessons of the war of 1971 really began to sink in ... In the beginning Pakistan had conducted annual 'Midlink' exercises from the late 1950s and was not particularly worried about the US and Soviet presence or for that matter of the Chinese presence in the region as it had secured good relationship with the USA.

According to Admiral HMS Chaudhari, the first Commander-in-Chief (Jan 1951- Feb 1958), the Pakistan Navy was conscious of its capability gap vis-a-vis the Indian Navy. But an absence of geographical depth, limited naval capability and financial constraints forced the Pakistan Navy to follow a defensive strategy. Notwithstanding that, it began to develop an effective naval strategy to counter the Indian naval threat and decided to go offensive in certain capabilities. It has been argued that Pakistan is not a sea power of necessity and in contrast to the Indian navy's strategy of sea control it has concentrated on sea denial and prevented its rival from maintaining naval supremacy.

The second factor, which has always been important for the Pakistan Navy is to take into account the likely changes in the international situation both globally and regionally that would have an impact on the Arabian Sea and the northern part of the Indian Ocean. It wants to keep the Karachi port safe and open for normal trade and provide normal protection to Pakistan's civil maritime interests. This may be the reason why Pakistan is developing Gwadar port off Karachi with the help of China in view of the development of missiles by both India and Pakistan that have a wider range and can cause havoc on each other's territories to a great extent.

Admiral Chaudhary has also been emphasizing upon day-to-day protection of Pakistan's EEZ till the time it can muster enough resources and know-how to exploit it. This factor becomes much more important in view of the international sea law regarding the continental shelf which was expected to come into force by 2005 and countries had to put forward their claims much before that for the continental shelves. This is reason why the Sir Creek dispute between India and Pakistan has once again surfaced and is proving to be difficult to be solved. This has led Pakistan to term 'Under the waters south of shoreline' as its fifth province i.e. the 'Extended Economic Zone.[10]

To fulfil all these three needs i.e. to counter the Indian Nay, to keep the port of Karachi open and to protect its EEZ, the Pakistan Navy has adopted the strategy of offensive defence. This means that Pakistan keeps its surface fleet along its shores in a sea denial role and the submarines in an offensive role.

The naval planners in Islamabad have remained preoccupied with the Indian threat of a naval blockade of Pakistan's seaports. As a matter of fact, the threat of a naval blockade finds a prominent place in Pakistan Navy's strategic thinking and tactical plans; this is primarily due to the past experiences during the 1965 and 1971 India Pakistan wars.

It may be noted that the Pakistan Navy is the only navy in South Asia that has the capability to fire anti-ship missiles (Harpoon) from submerged submarines. It also has superior anti-submarine and anti-surface warfare capability and also has air-to-sea missiles against enemy surface ships.

Admiral Aziz Mirza, the Pakistan Navy Chief, has dismissed the Indian capability to impose a naval blockade of Karachi and has threatened to launch missiles attacks on Kandla port in Gujarat if the Indian Navy blocked the port of Karachi in the event of a war. There are at least two reasons that have encouraged Admiral Abdul Aziz Mirza to dispel the threat of a naval blockade of Karachi; firstly, the Pakistan Navy is now developing alternative naval bases/ ports along the Makaran coast. It has overcome the constraints of "single channel, single naval base". Pakistan has begun the development of Ormara, Gwadar and Keti Bandar as new ports. Of these Ormara, which hosts the Jinnah Naval Base, is primarily designed as an alternative naval base while Keti Bandar would serve as the second commercial port. Gwadar, currently under development with Chinese assistance, is intended to be a commercial deep sea port as also a naval base.

The Admiral has however noted that the Pakistan Navy can protect only one of the sea lanes i.e. the Gulf trade route, the other two sea lanes i.e. the Red sea to Karachi and Far East to Karachi were at the mercy of the enemy and therefore the govt. needed to enhance its naval capability to undertake the protection of these sea lanes.

Sri Lanka

There are large islands and coral atolls in the Indian Ocean. Sri Lanka situated in the North Indian Ocean is a sovereign, independent state with the membership of the United Nations and other organizations like IOR-ARC, Commonwealth, SAARC, BIMSTEC, etc. The island has a land area of 64,740 Sq. kms and a coastline of 650 nautical miles. With the coming into force of the UN Law of the Seas (UNCLOS III) Sri Lanka has been entitled to 517,000 sq. kms of EEZ.[11] This makes the exploiting, building up and utilization of its maritime resources as well as saving them for future generations too very important for the country. Though a separate regime for the island states is yet to come into force due to the ongoing reframing of the continental shelf Sri Lanka may have extended EEZ.

Even though Sri Lanka is an island state it had no navy of its own till it acquired independence. Earlier it only had the Ceylon Royal Naval Volunteer Force, which was created under an ordinance in 1938. It was a small force and functioned only as an adjunct to the British force in the then Ceylon. After Ceylon was granted independence it formed the nucleus of the navy and was renamed the Royal Ceylon Navy (RCYN) and was finally established on 9 December 1950. After Ceylon changed its name to Sri Lanka, its navy was also renamed Sri Lanka Navy (SLN) on 22 May 1972.[12]

Even after Sri Lanka became independent its naval strategy remained a part of Britain's large Commonwealth strategy with the port of Trincomalee being the hub of that strategy and a base for the British Eastern Fleet. It was modernised keeping in view the necessity of keeping the sea-lanes safe and open, which needed mine clearance from the region.

The evolution of the naval policy of Sri Lanka was influenced by four variables:

1. The leaders of the newly independent state who most probably had not thought or even imagined a role for the

island republic in the near future were not willing to spend their scarce financial resources on the development of a conventional navy.

2. The leaders had only envisaged a preventive role for their navy i.e. to discourage and control the unauthorised movement of men and material between Sri Lanka and the coast of South India, and also to protect their fishing rights and prevent illegal human traffic between the two countries.
3. With the change in government the country's foreign policy also changed and now instead of being pro-west Sri Lanka became a non-aligned country, and
4. Britain also decided to shift its naval base from Trincomalee to Singapore in 1957 thus leaving the country to fend for itself.

At this time Sri Lanka did not try to upgrade or modernize its navy and it kept on working only as a custom's force. The need and necessity of having a modern navy was realised in the early 1970s when insurgency started in the tear drop shaped island. At this juncture the Sri Lankan navy slowly and gradually turned into an anti-insurgency navy instead of being a customs-oriented navy. It became more active as the Tamil insurgency became more serious after 1983. Now it started acquiring new ships and weapons to protect its national interests. This is necessary too keeping in view of the maritime security of the sea-lanes of this region that criss-cross the entire north central Indian Ocean.

South Africa

South Africa has both a South Atlantic and an Indian Ocean seaboard extending to 3000 kms. The main sea ports of Durban, East London and Port Elizabeth are on the Indian Ocean through which pass approximately 95% of the country's imports.[14] This explains the importance of the Indian Ocean for the Republic of South Africa.

Unlike the Atlantic and Pacific Oceans, the Indian Ocean is not open-ended. It is almost land-locked and has more choke points than gateways. The only open-ended entry or exit is located at the Southern tip of the African continent, the Cape of Good Hope in the Republic of South Africa. The very route which had brought Vasco-da-Gama to India, ushering in the era of Western dominance of Asia and Africa.[15] The Cape route dominated maritime history for several centuries before the Suez canal was opened and, even after that, it has retained its importance as only a choke free entry/exit for the Indian Ocean Region. Though this route is dear in terms of money and time, vessels carrying valuable/strategic cargo may have to take this route sooner or later looking at the growing trends/ incidents of piracy in the South East Asian Waters. Hence, the location of South Africa becomes no less strategic than that of India. The basic reason why India has always been remarked favourably by Africa even during the days of adverse relations between the two.

Australia

An important corner of the Indian Ocean is Australia, the other two being India and South Africa. The Indian Ocean borders 9,000 of the 12,000 miles of Australia's coastline. Still for a long time it was ignored and the Pacific was favoured in Australia's strategy, due to a variety of reason's e.g.,

1. Australia's Eastern tilt,
2. Great distance between its eastern and western flanks,
3. Its past experience and threat posed by Japan during World War II,
4. British presence in the Indian Ocean, and
5. USA - as a powerful friend and its considerable presence in the Indian Ocean (ANZUS-1951).[16]

A change in Australia's Pacific orientation came with Britain's announcement of its 'East of Suez' policy which replaced Pax-Britannica with Pax-Americana. Now, Australia was forced to consider the western as well as the eastern defence.

The Soviet entry in the Indian Ocean in 1968 also forced Australia to reconsider the security of its Indian Ocean island territories. As a result Australia supported the Indian Ocean Peace Zone proposal. In the post-cold war period Australia decided to make its navy a "two-ocean navy". This change was also reflected in its declaration of "Look West Policy"

Australia has commercial and strategic interests in Indian Ocean. Her main security interests in its eastern reaches are two, to protect its maritime approaches and ocean resources and the defence of the Cocoas and Christmas islands. Australia's interests were made explicit in its Government's foreign policy white paper, 'in the National interests', which was released in 1997. The white paper stated, the Indian Ocean Region will assume greater importance as the process of regional economic cooperation and development gathers pace with the countries of the Indian Ocean Region embarking on a path to further liberalisation of trade and investment in the region.

Japan

Geographically Japan is a pacific power and its principal economic, political and geo-strategic relationships are within and across the Pacific. The only factor that makes Japan interested in the Indian Ocean is that this waterbody separates Japan from the Middle West, which supplies fuel to its energy-hungry economy.

For a long time, Japan protected by the US - Japan security umbrella, has called its constitution a 'Peace' constitution that forbids any type of armed forces. But this situation is changing fast since the 9/11 terrorist attacks on the USA. Now the USA wants Japan to share its burden instead of being 'a free rider.' As a result Japan has started contributing logistical and other non-financial support to the naval operations in the Indian Ocean though a debate is still going on within the country to replace / renew or amend the Peace constitution.

Japan uses the Indian Ocean as its access to the Middle East from where comes the major supply of its crude oil (81.1% in 2000) in addition to coal, iron ore and oil products such as

LNG and heavy fuel oil. The Indian Ocean is also important as a shipping route for Japanese trade with European countries. Hence keeping the sea-lanes open is vital for Japan's economy, which may close down anytime due to myriad reasons especially around the various bottlenecks in the region.

Three straits provide crucial connection between the Indian Ocean and the Pacific and so are critical to the commercial shipping and trading routes of Japan and other East Asian nations. The Strait of Malacca is the main passage between the Indian Ocean and the South China Sea, and the Lombok and Sunda straits provide passage through the Indonesian archipelago. The Strait of Malacca and the South China Sea are recognised as the most important sea routes in the region because of the access that they give to the Indian Ocean through Southeast Asia. The US, Russia and China recognised the importance of these straits for their navies on their global and regional missions. Japan's principal concern is to satisfy its domestic economic needs since the Strait of Malacca is a vital lifeline for Japanese trade passing through the Indian Ocean.

Japan's main concern is only to keep these bottlenecks open so that it can have uninterrupted oil supply for its domestic economy. When this supply was threatened during the 1973 Middle East conflict, Japan had abandoned its neutrality and had taken pro-Arab position against the wishes of even the USA. During the Gulf war (1990) also Japan was accused of doing "too little and too late"

But 2001 changed all this under pressure from the USA. Japan sent its warships to provide "logistical support to the operating forces in Afghanistan under its newly passed (Oct. 2001) Anti Terrorism Special Measures Law, a first since the end of the Second World War.

France

France has constantly contested the idea that it is an external power in the Indian Ocean. The French claim to belong to the

Indian Ocean Region on the same footing as the other littoral countries. This claim is based on its regional territorial possessions, a cluster of islands: La Reunion island (2512 sq. km., larger than Mauritius: 1865 sq.km), the tiny island of Tromelin (450 km. east of Madagascar and 535 km. north of Reunion, a group of islands scattered along the Mozambique Channel; Mayotte (330 sq.km) a break-away island from the Comoros archipelago when the latter acceded to independence in 1976 and the Iles Eparse.

In the far south-west of the Indian ocean in the sub-Antarctic and the Antarctic region, there is another cluster of tiny islands, grouped together in the French Southern and Antarctic Territories; ile Amsterdam, ile Saint Paul, iles Crozet, Kerguelen archipelago, and a slice of the Antarctic continent called Land of Adelie.[18]

As a result of these overseas departments and territories, France is territorially present in two of the four zones of the Indian ocean (the Persian Gulf, The Eastern African Coast and adjoining islands, the Indo-Australian arc and the Antarctic and adjoining islands), and more significantly, the French 200 mile EEZ in the Indian Ocean (2.5 million km) is seven times larger than the EEZ of metropolitan France, and also larger than the Indian EEZ.

France occupied the second position in possessing EEZ i.e. 2,083,400 sq. nautical miles next to the US which possesses 2,831,400 nm.[19]

"France without its overseas territories would occupy only the forty - fifth position amongst the maritime powers, coming way behind South Korea and slightly ahead of Libiya."[20]

The EEZ of France is at the crossroads of three major maritime trading routes: the Persian Gulf / the Atlantic Ocean, Africa / Southeast Asia, Africa / Australia. These possessions are elements of France's assertion of its world power rank and justify its permanent military presence in the region. On this basis France did try to gain membership of the IOR-ARC but it was only given the status of a 'dialogue partner' in 2001 and hence remains the only European colonial presence in the Indian Ocean since the British withdrawal from the area.

French defence policy in the Indian Ocean evolves first from its immediate national interests i.e.

1. The protection of its overseas department and territories,
2. Of the French nationals abroad,
3. Of its two hundred miles of EEZ,
4. Of its international responsibilities resulting from bilateral agreements and as a permanent member of the United Nations Security Council and;
5. For implementation of UN resolutions and the respect for Sea Law Conventions and to protect its sanctuary (Metropolitan).

It means monitoring the main SLOC's and straits, going into military action if the need so arises, asserting its presence vis-a-vis other littoral states by regularly calling on each of them, conducting joint naval exercises and activities, frequently interacting with other allied western navies operating in the region and overseeing the economic activities in the French EEZ.

Thus it becomes evident that, "Islands have made France the second largest maritime power" in the world. [21]

Madagascar, Mauritius, the Comoros and Mayotte are very close to the Mozambique Channel, a critical choke point for southbound oil tanker traffic. After the loss of its military base in Madagascar in 1974, France found it indispensable to develop its bases at Djibouti, Reunion and Mayotte, to continue to keep the Mozambique Channel under its surveillance.

France sought to strengthen its presence in the Indian Ocean by developing its base at Reunion, which is of immense strategic importance to France because it lies on the oil route and the sea/air lanes of communication between Southern

Africa and the Far East. Without its presence in Reunion, it felt that it would be difficult to have control over the other island states which are under its control in the region. [22]

Varuna-2004

To enhance cooperation in the region France has also started conducting joint naval exercises in the Indian Ocean, the latest being Varuna-2004. It has held 11 such exercises in the past five years with India. Varuna, the 10 days exercise involving over 5000 personnel, a dozen warships, backed up by helicopters, fighter jets and long-range maritime patrol air craft, began off the coast of Oman on April 6 and continued till the 12 warships reached the Indian Coast. Aimed at achieving inter-operatibility i.e. the crucial ability of two different forces to operate together. The exercise was successful in its aim.

China

Historically China looked only as far as the Great wall in its national security policy, which was entirely defensive in nature. The national security objectives outlined by Mao were: sovereignty, reunification of lost territories, defence of its borders and modernization. Deng Xiao Ping had slightly changed emphasis on these objectives i.e. sovereignty, defence of China reunification of lost territories and modernization. Deng also made the peaceful settlement of off-shore disputes a part of China's national security programme and aimed for the joint administration of islands in areas of conflict.

With the changing times China's security objectives have also undergone a sea change. Now these are described as, "to consolidate national defence, resist foreign aggression, safeguard state sovereignty, maritime interests and rights and maintain national unity and security." Maritime rights and interests represent China's right and claim to new waters in the oceans, new territories and their riches above and below the water, which is very significant looking at China's history and claim over other territories.

In terms of both its history and geography, Mainland China has essentially been a maritime country. With its 18000 km mainland coastline and 14,000 km. island coastline, China constitutes the single largest maritime landmass in the Asia-Pacific. Also as early as 'by the fifth century B.C. China had started to have an army of ships that could engage in naval operations.

China was an original signatory to the UN Convention on the Seas 1982, which it ratified in 1996. As a result China has obtained access to the natural wealth of its three million sq. km. EEZ as agreed upon under the UN convention. Until this convention was ratified and became effective in 1992, the PRC had legal authority only over 3,80,000 sq. km. of its island and territorial waters, which it claimed up to the 12 nautical mile limit. If one were to add to this China's island sea of Bo Hai, its maritime area will comprise about 4.7 million sq. km. [23]

The UN has in fact added a new category called the "Developmental Zone" to China's waters. Since 1991, Chinese ships have been sanctioned to replace valuable seabed resources in an additional 105,000 sq. km. developmental zone in the international and waters in the Pacific Ocean.

"According to Liu Zhenhuan who is the director of the navy's Military Research Institute (in Beijing), despite having the world's fourth largest coastline, fifth largest continental shelf (in area) and tenth largest EEZ compared to worldwide ratios between the maritime space under a nations jurisdiction and its land area which arrearages 94:100, China's ratio stands only at 30:100 which is less than even one third of the existing world average.

It was due to the efforts of Liu Huaqing, who occupies a unique position in the history of the growth of the PLAN, and is likened to be the Chinese version of Alfred Thayer Mahan for his emphasis on sea power that China was launched on to the world stage in its maritime dimensions. As a commander of the PLAN in the 1980's, he revised several of the maritime strategic principles of the country. He not only set an expansion programme for the PLAN till 2040 but also, by several inputs to the CCP leadership, was instrumental in the strategic shift in the defence strategy of the country towards a blue water navy .[24] Now, it is generally believed that China will be the trend-setter or the pace-setter for this region.

Impressive economic growth, a large merchant marine, the growing ship building industry and maritime trade including China's claims over the South China sea are an indication to the fact that China is fast emerging as an important maritime power in the international system. Some factors that have contributed to this change in China's policy are:

1. In China hinterland rail and road communications are inadequate resulting in greater pressure on maritime transport. China also wants to ensure an uninterrupted flow of energy requirements to fuel the growing economy together with unhindered access to the sources of raw materials and markets for its finished products. For this it has to ensure safety of SLOC's.
2. Import of crude oil has increased China's dependence on maritime trade resulting in its enhanced interest in the Bay of Bengal and the Andaman Sea. This dependence on import of crude oil is expected to grow in future which will have to coincide with the growing Chinese presence on these waters.
3. The questions of territorial sovereignty that lies at the core of China's claims to its maritime jurisdiction over the whole of South China Sea will make it an Indian Ocean Country. Based on various arguments of historicity, usage and legality, China virtually lays claims on the whole of South China Sea. If these claims get accepted, China will not only have control over vast resources (including oil) of South China Sea it will also get an extended reach in the Indian and the Pacific Ocean and will be able to control the important sea lanes of this region.
4. China's Indian Ocean policy is largely dependent on its fears and suspicions of the US and Soviet presence (during

the cold war period) in the ocean which it took as its own 'encirclement' by the enemy. After the end of the cold war, the shrinking presence of the US and Russia has provided China enough space to manoeuvre in these waters.

China's Indian Ocean policy is also directly linked to its perceptions and problems with India. Since the Indo Chinese war of 1962 China has been concentrating on the theme that - India is trying to become a hegemon in this region and China will not allow it to treat the Indian Ocean as its 'own ocean'. It is to counter India's such imagined claims over the Indian Ocean that China is developing close relations with all the countries in the region whose relations with India have been problematic e.g. Pakistan, Sri Lanka, Myanmar, etc.

To fulfil its aim and objectives in the IOR China has been trying to become active in multilateral organizations like IOR-ARC, the Shanghai five, APEC and ARF. As a result IOR-ARC accepted China as its dialogue partner in its special session at Oman during January 22-23, 2000.[25] Given the fact that geographically China is not a state in the Indian Ocean, this decision of IOR-ARC leaves no doubt to the fact that members of this forum attach great importance to China's interests, interactions and influence in the IOR.

Japan, Vietnam, ASEAN, Australia, France, India and South Africa, all have been expanding their ocean-based interactions providing a good example for China to do likewise. The changing patterns of US-Japan security arrangements have also provided a boost to China's efforts and have increased its zeal to expand its own sphere of influence in time. China also wants to check the entry of Taiwan in these waters as a part of its long-standing policy and has been successful so far.

Of late China has increased its presence in the Indian Ocean and now has started joint naval exercises with India as well. This process had started in early 1986 when for the first time the Chinese had sailed in these waters and had made port calls to Bangladesh, Pakistan and Sri Lanka. In November 1993 a Chinese military training ship made a port visit to Bombay but this did not stop China from making mysterious forays into the Indian waters. In August - 1994, the Indian Coast Guard had captured three Chinese trawlers in the Andaman seas, one of these was equipped with modern electronic monitoring gear for surveillance, which appears to be a well-known Chinese technique in building up its naval presence. Similar incidents happened in the Sri Lankan waters, and China's support to Cocoas base (Myanmar), Gwadar base (Pakistan) is not unknown to anybody. Hence, it becomes explicit that China's friendly gestures and interactions continue to be guided by China's strategic vision and therefore must be corroborated with China's literature on strategic affairs. General Zhao Zanqui, the then commander of China's Academy of Military Sciences, is often quoted as saying that China would extend its naval operations farther than the South and East China Seas to check attempts by India to dominate the Indian ocean,[26] and this about sums up China's interests and strategies in the India Ocean.

Of the hundred and odd Choke points in the world today, The Indian Ocean is one of the 16 most important strategic sea passes through which heavy maritime trade is conducted. Over 300 ships traverse the Indian Ocean on a daily basis. Each year over $ 200 billion worth of crude oil passes through the straits of Hormuz and $ 60 billion worth through the Malacca straits. About 40 super tankers pass through the nine-degree channel (near Lakshadweep) every day. This is enough to show how important, the Indian Ocean is for the power (Energy/oil) hungry world. Even if we ignore all other important factors, then too only the transport of oil through the Indian Ocean can explain the growing presence of the regional and extra regional navies in the Indian Ocean region which is bound to increase by the day in times to come.

References

1. Unnithan, Sandeep, "Ship-Shape", India Today, May 12, 2003.
2. Palwar, AKS, "International Fleet- Review", Journal of Indian Ocean Studies, Vol. 8, No. 3, December 2000, pp. 248-252.

3. Sukumaran, R. "Operationalizing Gorshkov", Strategic Analysis, Vol. 28, No. 01, January-March, 2004. pp. 37-53.
4. Prasad, Ravi VS, "In Need of Sea Change", The Hindustan Times, 21 November 2002.
5. "India's Largest Naval Base Afloat, "The Times of India, 1 June, 2005.
6. "Kadamb Nausainik Adda Rashtra Ko Samarpit", Rajasthan Patrika, 1 June, 2005.
7. Singh, S.K. "Towards A Cohesive Policy of Indian Ocean", The Times of India, 24 September, 1991.
8. Till, Geoffrey, "International Maritime Trends and Indian Ocean in 21st Century", Journal of Indian Ocean Studies, Vol. 9 No. 2, Aug. 2001, pp. 150-166.
9. Sakhuja, Vijay, "Pakistan's Naval Strategy: Past and future", Strategic Analysis. Vol. 26. No. 4. October-December 2002, pp. 493-507.
10. Naqvi, M.B., "Indian Ocean and Our Naval Defence", Defence Journal, Vol. XVI, No.6, 1990, pp. 25-31, Karachi, Pakistan.
11. Chandra, Satish, "Indian Ocean Islands and Littorals- Conflict and Cooperation", Journal of Indian Ocean Studies, Vol. 9, No. 01, April 2001, pp. 1-6.
12. Sin, K.R., "Sri Lanka- Evolution of Naval Strategy", Journal of Indian Ocean Studies, Vol. 10, No.1, April. 2004, pp. 91-99.
13. *Ibid*.
14. Roy, Mihir, "South Africa; An Emerging Player in the Indian Ocean," Journal of Indian Ocean Studies, Vol. 2. No. 01, November, 1994. pp. 55-63.
15. Ramamurthi, T.G., "India-South Africa and the Indian Ocean", Journal of Indian Ocean Studies, Vol. 1, No.2 March, 1994.
16. Kaur, Kuldeep," Australia's Changing Orientation from Pacific to Indian Ocean", Journal of Indian Ocean Studies, Vol. 8, No. 3, December 2000, pp. 203-216.
17. Jain, Purendra, "Japan's Interest in Indian Ocean", Journal of Indian Ocean Studies, Vol II, No. 01, April 2003, pp. 8-23.

18. Boquerat, Gilles, "French Interests in Indian Ocean Region and the Relevance of India", Journal of Indian Ocean Studies, Vol. II, No. 9, Aug. 2003. pp. 234-246.
19. Jacobson, John L. (ed.) "Ocean Development and International Law". Vol. 26, No. 3, July-Sep, 1995, Taylor and Francis Ltd. London.
20. Saxena, Jyotsna, "France and the Indian Ocean", Lancer International, New Delhi. 1991.
21. Raju, A. Subrtamanyan, "French Economic and Strategic Interests in the Indian Ocean Region-1975, 1990", Journal of Indian Ocean Studies, Vol. 5, No. 11, November, 1997, pp. 21-34.
22. Young, P. Lewis, "French Forces: A Major Factor in Indian Ocean Security", Asian Defence Journal, April 1986, pp. 64-71.
23. Singh, Swaran, "Continuity and Change in China's Maritime strategy", Strategic Analysis, Vol. XXIII, No. 9, December 1999, pp. 1493-1508.
24. Kondapalli, Srikanth. " Chinese Navy: Political Work and Personnel", Strategic Analysis, vol. XXIII, No. 10, Jan. 2000, pp. 1749-1768.
25. Singh, Swaran, "China's Indian Ocean Policy-Complications vs. Ambitions", Journal of Indian Ocean Studies, Vol. 8, No. 1-2, August 2000, pp. 65-78.
26. "China Plans to Build up Navy", The Hindustan Times, 13 January 1993.

8

Indo-US relations and prospects of peace in the Indian Ocean region

The Indian Ocean plays an important role in world politics and due to its geo-strategic importance, vital maritime resources and sea lines of communications (SLOC's), it has acquired immense importance in recent times. Political instability, economic underdevelopment, wide differences in perceptions of littoral countries, conflicting national interests and mutual suspicions make the countries of the region highly susceptible not only to the evil designs of the great powers who want to exploit this region for their own vested interests but also to the growing menace of terrorism and smuggling of drugs, gold and human beings across the sovereign borders which pose a threat not only to regional peace but also to the peace and security of the whole world.

In the post cold war era the United States of America as the only super power (!) in a multipolar world and India as the only strong regional naval presence (aiming to become a blue water navy, having realized the importance of maritime power a little two late) have become the important actors in the Indian Ocean Region. Hence, relations between these two countries and the degree of ease and cooperation between these two will have a great impact or prospects of peace in the region in times to come. Though the other regional and extra-regional navies e.g. the French, Japanese, Chinese, South African, Australian and those of South East Asian nations too are becoming more active in the Indian ocean, it is the Indian and US navies that will play the deciding role in the near future. This makes study of Indo-US naval cooperation much more important.

India in Indian Ocean - Due to its strategic location, vast coast line (6100 kms of coastline and 1400 kms of island and rock territories to protect, not to mention the vast Exclusive Economic Zone) and a large number of islands, both inhabited and uninhabited, in the Bay of Bengal and the Arabian Sea, development, deployments, bases and probable flash points in the Indian Ocean have always been very important for the safety, security and protection of the national interests of the country.

Though this fact was ignored for a long time (despite suitable warnings from Gen. K.B. Vaidya, K.M Pannikkar and the like to this effect), the sea frontiers were not taken care of properly. The navy was not given its due share of importance and policy makers, academicians, politicians and masses all remained blissfully unaware of our sea frontiers and unduly preoccupied with the land frontiers (specially with the North Eastern sector and the Himalayas). Now the situation is changing rapidly and the country has started paying attention to its maritime security and interests.

How did this change of perception come about? History has taught India two bitter lessons firstly, that the neglect of maritime power can culminate in a termination of sovereignty, and secondly, that it takes decades to revert to being a considerable maritime power after a period of neglect and decline. These forgotten lessons of history were remembered once again in 1971 with full force when India had to involve itself in a war with Pakistan over the question of liberation of the then East Pakistan, now Bangladesh. During this period the Indian Ocean had become a theatre of war and had witnessed unprecedented naval presence of both the super powers, the then Soviet Union and the United State of America. Though India did win the war and a new nation emerged on the world political map India had to seek the erstwhile Soviet

Union's help and support in its endeavours that lead to many questions being raised regarding India's non-aligned status.

Immediately after 1971, the oil crisis of 1973 once again brought to the forefront importance of keeping the SLOC's and trade routes open: "**ALWAYS AND FOR ALL**". More recently the terrorist attacks of September 2000 on the United States of America have brought the non-traditional threats to maritime security of a state to the fore and re-emphasised cooperation among sovereign democratic and peace loving countries to deal with such threats.

Maritime Interests of India - As far as the maritime interests of India are concerned, they imply freedom of navigation for shipping, the enforcement of laws of the sea and, more importantly, it comprises the entire spectrum of shipping.

1. In India merchant ships carry 95% of the country's trade; therefore it becomes essential to protect its merchant shipping.

2. Sub-continental India has a coastline of 6,100 kilometres with the island territories of Lakshadweep and the Andaman and Nicobar islands (598 islands near shore 572 in the Andaman and Nicobar group and 27 in Lakshadweep group) adding another 14,00 kilometres. This coastline harbours eleven major, twenty intermediate and 144 minor ports, to be protected and taken care of.

3. The country's sea lanes are economically important and serve as vital sea borne trade routes through the Indian Ocean, nowadays infested with pirates and their activities.

4. High value assets in the form of offshore oil and the vast potential of mineral and seabed resources in the waters surrounding it add another important dimension to its maritime interests.

5. India also has fishing interests in its EEZ that are vital for its economy as well as for food supply for its citizens.

6. India is aiming to become a blue water navy. For fulfilling this aim it will have to have a strong naval presence in the region.

7. India can become active in the East Asian Indian Ocean Region by increasing its escort operations and thus enhance its cooperation with the growing economies of South East Asia, and last but not the least,

8. India sees the presence of Chinese and Pakistani navies, and their ever-growing presence and cooperation as a threat to its security and national interests, not without undue reasons too, looking at the bitter historical experiences it has had with both its neighbours.

In addition to the traditional threats, non-traditional threats too have become graver for the security and national interests of the country. Sea piracy, narco-terrorism, illegal migration and emigration, human security, terrorism and very rapid depletion of maritime resources (both living and non-living), environmental pollution, the presence of extra-regional navies and lack of cooperation among the littoral countries make the situation worse, and cooperation with a big power is essential to protect country's national interests. After having lost the erstwhile Soviet Union (due to its disintegration) as a close ally and in the changed world scenario who could fulfil that position better than the United States of America? Thus the newfound bonhomie between the two countries is attributed to the following reasons:

1. Loss of Soviet Union as a dependable ally.

2. A new role for India in the Indian Ocean and its increasing expertise in the maritime affairs as evident from the 'Pioneer Status' granted to it in the Indian Ocean.

3. Indian navy's aim of becoming a blue water navy can be achieved by purchasing advance equipment from the USA and if possible with transfer of technology from the same quarters.

4. Security concerns of India as China and Pakistan are increasing their presence in the ocean and cooperation between the two is also on a roller coaster ride.
5. To increase expertise in safeguarding its economic and territorial interests which require greater exposure to the advanced technology of the USA.
6. To lend a helping hand to its friends and allies against sea pirates as happened when India rescued the Japanese ship 'Alondra Rainbow' which was hijacked.[1]
7. Moreover in the post-cold war world the focus of international politics has shifted from the Atlantic-Pacific to the Pacific- Indian Ocean.[2]
8. In a way this can also be called the new silk route as the most important energy resources are located here and the area is surrounded by booming economies.
9. Looking at the enhanced cooperation between India and the South East Asian countries due to its' Look East Policy,' a greater Indian presence in the region may prove to be very beneficial in the long run

United States of America in the Indian Ocean

Apart from a relatively modest amount of trade with the littoral states of the Indian Ocean, the United States' interests did not really begin to grow until the late twenties, when the Americans put a foot inside the Middle Eastern petroleum tent. Even after their entry into the region the American presence in the region was not a significant one as:

1. Its interests were being looked after by its close ally the United Kingdom, who had made the Indian Ocean virtually a British lake.
2. In the US eyes prime importance was of the Atlantic, North Pacific and the Mediterranean; the Indian Ocean came after all these.

3. Due to regional security pacts with the Northern tier countries (Turkey, Iran, Pakistan etc), it really was not much concerned or bothered with the developments in this region.

This situation changed when the British decided to withdraw from the Indian Ocean in the wake of the Second World War, declared their 'East of Suez' policy and established the 'British Indian Ocean Territory (BIOT). Now the theory of power vacuum was propounded for the Indian Ocean and the United States of America decided to step in, in the place vacated by the British to protect its own national interests by increasing its naval presence and establishing a permanent naval base, Diego Garcia, in the strategically vital Chagos Archipelago.

Ever since this region of turmoil has witnessed the ever-growing US presence in the region. But, it was the terrorist attack of 9/11 that made the super power realize the importance of regional cooperation if it wanted to protect its vital national interests in the region. The US interests in the Indian ocean region, that make cooperation with India essential can be broadly defined as:

1. It can effectively deal with the growing trends of terrorism with India's help, as India itself is a victim of terrorism and willing to cooperate.
2. With India on its side the US presence would be more readily acceptable to other regional countries.
3. India can co-share its naval responsibilities in the East Asian Region.
4. The Indian Ocean would provide a much needed training area to the American navy as they have no other facilities between the Persian Gulf and South East Asia.
5. It needs to protect the Gulf oil passing through the vital sea-lanes of this region, which is necessary for its economy.
6. It can hope to curve the growing Russian and Chinese naval presence in the region by projecting India as a regional power and a force to reckon with. The United

States with its 11650 nautical miles of coastline on two great oceans and the Gulf of Mexico has always been a sea-faring nation. Its history, present and destiny, all are closely linked to the wide waters of the earth. Its national security too is directly and immediately dependent on the events in the international sea.

It is an irony that both India and the United States have comparatively ignored their sea power for a long time despite ample warnings to this effect. But now, both the nations have once again become aware of this lopsided view of their national security and interests. A change in their perceptions has now become obvious which is also reflected in their changing bilateral relations.

Indo-US Relations

Indo-US relations have always been on ups and downs. For the convenience of study (particularly, for this project) these can be divided into various categories like:

1. Indo-US relations during the cold war era.
2. Indo-US relations in the post cold war era.
   a. Indo-US relations prior to 9/11, and
   b. Indo-US relations after 9/11.

Relations between any two countries cover the broad spectrum of political, diplomatic, trade and economic, cultural and agricultural, scientific and technological, educational and defence relations which are interdependent and have a great influence on each other. No single study can cover all these at a go, so in this study an attempt is made to limit the discussion to Indo-US naval cooperation, which is reflected in their joint exercises.

Indo-US defence relationship has always been an extremely sensitive issue. During the cold war years the United States looked upon India with a sense of caution because it had a close alliance with the former Soviet Union. During that period the United States had developed a few mechanisms to control the export of advanced technologies and dual use goods as these could be used by their all-time adversary the Soviet Union. Even after the end of the cold war this caution in the US policy continued and bilateral cooperation between the two countries remained at a very low level specially as far as the defence and nuclear technologies were concerned. In all other areas like agriculture, engineering and even space technologies, which included information technology later on, cooperation between the two countries was much higher.

The end of the cold war in the 1990s coincided with the liberalization of Indian economy. As a result the Clinton administration identified India as one of the 10 major emerging markets. The high water mark of the improved relationship was the strategic partnership, consummated during President Clinton's successful visit in 2000. As the Indo-US relations started improving once again, opportunities for strategie cooperation also grew. This betterment of relations was a direct result of a desire to exploit India's vast markets. As a result the United States was forced to lift the economic sanctions that were imposed on India in the aftermath of its nuclear explosion of May 1998. At that time severe restrictions were placed on India for not following the US directives and all joint exercises, including the Malabar exercises, were stopped and relations between the two had plummeted to the deepest low. While the United States was trying to make India follow its line, India was trying to establish itself as a regional power by adopting an independent stand on the issue of signing the Comprehensive Test Ban Treaty (CTBT) by claiming a place among the Nuclear weapons power states and projecting itself as a rightful claimant of a permanent member's seat in the United Nations.

At this very time the United States was taken aback by terrorist attacks on its own territory. Now the threat of terrorism was made real by this unfortunate incident and the United States was compelled to fight the evil of terrorism. It soon realized that to fight with the growing menace of terrorism is not an easy task and despite being a super power it needed to have regional allies to face the situation and effectively deal with it. Even the United States did not want to put much burden on its own economy and simultaneously wanted to show the world that it was not alone in fighting the menace of terrorism, that it was a **'civilizational conflict'** and a country like India was supporting it in its war on the 'Axis of Evil'. Hence the post 9/11 backlash by the United States altered the entire strategic spectrum in the Indian Ocean Region. The direct campaign against the terrorist organization Al Qaeda brought the extra-regional into the regional powers once again (after the Gulf war) and reestablished the belief that establishing peace in the Indian Ocean Region is essentially an extra-regional function.

In the changed circumstances India recognized the US presence in the Indian Ocean and also accepted it while the United States endorsed India's status as a regional power. Driven by their own separate motives, cooperation in the Indian Ocean region had become a necessity for both India and the United States of America. Now the American security discourse in the region was dominated by the issues of non-proliferation, human rights, terrorism, free-trade, etc. Moreover, new concerns had emerged in the form of 'civilization conflicts' between the west and the orient. This new situation required the United States to deal with fundamentalist groups, narco-terrorism piracy on the sea, 'rogue states,' and the United states did not want any direct intervention and if essential wanted to minimize it to the absolute minimum. This required a strong regional ally who would take care of the American interests in the region, make its presence wherever necesstary more acceptable and less obvious by lending a helping hand, and no other country than India could fulfil these objectives as easily and as readily because due to its own reasons India too was looking for a friend and close ally to step in the place vacated by the erstwhile Soviet Union and help it realise its long cherished ambition of becoming a regional power, defeating similar claims put forward by its adversaries like Pakistan and China. All these factors put together paved the way for the enhanced cooperation between the United States and India.

Towards Cooperation

The stage for growing cooperation between the sole super power in a multipolar world, the United states of America, and the regional power in the making India, was set in, in the aftermath of the cold war. The unprecedented, unimagined and even unwanted and uncalled for situation of the sudden collapse of a super power improved the prospects of a genuine and warm cooperation between the United States and India, two largest democracies of the world that have a lot in common as well as a lot to disagree upon. India lent its support to the international coalition (led by the United States) against Iraq in 1991 and American aircraft refueled in India on their way to the Gulf. Nothing could be more in contrast with the situation in 1971 when the US Enterprize had entered the Bay of Bengal. Moreover Indian troops patrolled with the American army in peacekeeping operations in Somalia (1992) and the navies of both the countries conducted joint naval exercises. This was in line with the United States' policy in the post cold war era, which focussed its naval doctrine towards regional challenges. The white paper on US maritime strategy **from the sea**[3] (1992) stressed the withdrawal of forces from overseas bases and underlined joint military operations and cooperation of services in the twenty first century. The US Navy's abandonment of its traditional blue water strategy in favour of focus on the world's coastline or littoral is described as **'forward from the sea**[4]**'**. According to this strategy, Marine Expeditionary Force (MEF) was to undertake many missions that would include long range operations and early forcible entry to enable the arrival of follow-on forces. The key to such an enabling mission was domination and exploitation of the littoral battle space during the earliest phases of hostilities[5]. The three components of the forward forces are peacetime engagement, deterrence, conflict prevention and ability to fight and win wars.[6]

The Navy's operational concept of March 1997 had stressed the US ability to carry out swiftly and effectively any naval missions, joint or coalition, and to prevail decisively over any opposing force, while the joint vision 2010 of the armed forces provided the template for joint combat operations. The Cooperative Defence Initiative (CDI) of the Clinton administration in April 2000 embodied the US strategy to consolidate its role in the Middle East through bases and extra-military presence in the Western Indian Ocean Region. Admiral Van Clark, chief of naval operations, had outlined in 2002 the central tenets of the vision. It divides the navy's capabilities into three categories: Sea Strike, Sea Basing and Sea Shield.[7] President Bush during his recent address at the US Naval Academy said, "I am committed to building a future that is defined less by size and more by mobility and swiftness, one that is easier to deploy and sustain, one that relies more heavily on stealth, precision weaponry and technologies."[8] This makes it clear that the US Navy's strategic objective is to influence directly and decisively events ashore from the sea in the Indian Ocean region.

All this was in line with India's changed perception of the newly found Indo-US maritime understanding matured into collaborative exercises. Shortly after the Gulf war the navies of both the countries conducted a two-day exercise in the Indian ocean in May 1992, a twenty-day joint exercise on maritime counter terrorism and peace keeping operations in Ratnagiri in September 1994. Another exercise was conducted on the Malabar Coast in May 1995 and in February 2001 the United States took part in the first ever biggest multi-lateral exercise in the ocean hosted by India in the Arabian sea joined by 19 countries. The United States' president pronounced in January 2002 his country's plan to wage a universal war against international terrorism. The so-termed 'Bush Doctrine' declared Asia as the' Axis of Evil' which bred terrorism and Islamic fundamentalism and favoured 'preemptive strikes' to deal with such acts of terrorism. To fulfil his objective the United States required a regional ally. Now the stage, which was fully set by the Clinton administration in the form of 'strategic partnership', was ready to be played upon by the Bush administration. The Vajpayee-Bush Summit meeting of November 2001 paved the way for future acts of collaboration and co-operation, and close military defence ties between the two countries began to take shape.

The pace of this defence cooperation was rather unprecedented and comprehensive, short only of formalizing a bilateral military pact. The Defence Policy Group (DPG), the apex body (that met in December, 2001) consisting of senior officials from both the countries identified three core areas of long term joint defence programme, i.e.

1. Military to military cooperation.
2. Defence trade and technology transfer, and
3. Institutional structures for strategic dialogue

At the end of the meeting the DPG's joint statement announced that both the countries share strategic interests in 'Asia and beyond'. ' Since then DPG has been meeting every year alternately in India and the United States and looks for new vistas of cooperation.

Since the first ever DPG meeting, Indo-US naval interaction has reached new heights. The US aircraft carrier USS Carl Vinson docked at Mumbai during its anti-Taliban operations followed by the guided missile cruiser USS O'kane and USS Antietam. A multinational Search And Rescue (SAR) exercise involving battleship USS John C Stennis and INS Godavari was held in December 2001. USS John Young and USS O'Brien visited Chennai in November 2001 followed by the seventh command USS Blue Ridge in February 2002 which lasted the Indo-US defence executive meetings.[9]

Malabar Exercises: The joint naval exercises conducted in May 1992 were the first between India and the United States in more than three decades, and started a series of future exercises by the same name. It was 'a round the clock exercise that involved four war ships: INS Rajput and INS Gomati, USS Vandegrift and USS David R. Ray. This exercise mainly consisted of general drills and manoeuvres, replenishments at seas, communications, and search and rescue operations. On the whole it was an attempt to test each other's naval capabilities, timing and response.[10]

Malabar - 2 was conducted in May 1995 for two days and Malabar 3 was held in 1996 for three weeks. These exercises provided an insight into the high sea naval operations of one another and helped augment naval synergies. This exercise also included a US Navy flotilla including two destroyers, a frigate, a couple of submarines that constituted a nuclear powered anti-submarine helicopters and PC-3 Orion maritime reconnaissance aircraft along with a host of support vessels. The Indian side was joined by a destroyer, a submarine, several helicopters and Tripolov long range maritime survey planes. This exercise was viewed as a close naval defence cooperation in training and logistics.

Then came the nuclear explosions of May 1998 by India followed by Pakistan and the whole security gamut changed in the subcontinent. As a result relations between India and the United States of America once again became strained, naval exercises between the two countries were suspended and the United States imposed heavy economic sanctions on India. After the terrorist attack of 9/11 on the United States the situation once again changed. In October 2000 the United States tanker USS Cole was attacked by two Arab men, which raised concerns about maritime security. In this changed scenario, as earlier mentioned, the United States felt the need of regional cooperation, and naval exercises between India and the United States were resumed again.

Malabar-4 was the longest and largest Indo-US joint naval exercise. This was undertaken from September 29 to October 03, 2002 and nearly 4000 personnel from the Indian navy and 750 from the US navy participated in these exercises. The warships that took part in these exercises included Ticonderoga class guided missiles cruiser, USS Chancellorville, the sprunance class destroyer USS Paul F. Foster and a PC 3 Orion maritime reconnaissance aircraft. From the Indian side the latest INS Delhi, INS Gomati, a Godavari class frigate, a SSK class submarine, INS Shankul and a tanker INS Aditya participated.[11] Later, at the end of 2002 both the navies conducted Search and Rescue (SAR) operations. These operations were conceived in 2001 during the commander-in-chief US Pacific Command, Admiral Blair's visit to Mumbai. Soon after, USS Hewitt, a US navy ship while transiting the Arabian sea sought India's help for 'medical casualty', evacuation of a sailor who was treated on board the ship. According to Admiral Blair, the life -saving exercise was the beginning of a new chapter in the bilateral naval cooperation.[12]

To protect merchant shipping in the pirate-infested Malacca straits and to lessen the burden on either country, both the countries decided to have their vessels escorted through these areas on a shared basis. This decision resulted in 'Operation Enduring freedom 2001.'[13] Both the countries divided responsibilities of escorting their high value vessels on a six month basis. The Indian ships Sukanya and Sharda escorted the US ships (April-September 2002) through the sensitive Malacca straits by taking over these responsibilities from USS Cowpens. In September-October 2002, two Indian frigates and a destroyer exercised with the US Navy's destroyers and a nuclear submarine.[14] 'In May 2002, the US had agreed to consider the Indian request to extend patrols from Malacca to Hormuz as part of the Indo-US naval cooperation. But later on it turned down the proposal due to 'operational jurisdiction constraints' as the Gulf falls under the US central command (USCENTCOM), while India is covered by the Pacific command (PACOM).'[15] Still the momentum of cooperation kept rising and 'Indian experts participated in a missile defence game in Colorado in 2002 and a missile defence workshop was held in Delhi in 2004. India was also invited to observe' Roving sands' missile defence exercises in the US[16]. The Indian navy was also engaged by the Bush administration in the 'Team Challenge', a multinational naval exercise held in the Philippines in the summer of 2002. It was the first ever exercise by the Indian navy in the East Asian Security Zone, which is considered China's primary security domain.[17]

Malabar 2003. Held from October 5-10, Codenamed MALABAREX, fifth in the series, these exercises were held in 2003. Understanding each other's 'Operating Philosophy' was the theme of these exercise. Malabar was the Indian Navy's biggest ever joint exercises with the US navy. 'Taking part in the exercises, besides the Brahmputra and the Chosin, were the Indian Navy's guided missile frigate (Godavari class) INS Ganga, the diesel electric powered Shishumar (Howaldtswerke Deutshe Werft HDW 209) class submarine INS Shalki and the replenishment tanker/force multiplier INS Shakti. The US flotilla had, besides the Ticonderoga class Chosin, the Arleigh Burke class destroyer USS Fitzgerald, the Los Angeles class nuclear powered submarine USS Pasadaen, and the 62000 tone oil tanker USS Chesapeake. Two US P3C Orion long-range maritime patrol aircraft (LRMPS) also took part in these exercises.'[18]

The flurry of exercises in the Arabian Sea also provided a show window for US military equipment that India has been eyeing for long. For the Indian navy, the US made aircraft Orion (which took part in these exercises) is the answer to augment its graying fleet of a dozen Russian made LRMPS and it has opened negotiations for buying eight of them.[19] At this time India was trying to purchase defence equipment from the United States. The US had planned to sell India four more fire finder AN/TPQ-37 counter battery radars adding to the eight already purchased by India in a $ 146 million (Rs 672 crore) deal, the largest between the two countries in four decades. India was also looking at the US made Patriot -3 anti-ballistic missile defence system and wanted strategic assets like Israel's Phalcon early warning radar system and Green Pine anti-ballistic missile defence radars. Joint naval exercises between the two countries can also provide greater access to US arms and technology for the Indian navy.

Absent from the exercises despite persistent US requests were the Indian navy's Russian built Sindhughosh (Kilo class) submarines also called type 877 EKM or Blade hole because of their silent operation. Explained an officer, 'The Americans did bait us to get one of our kilo class subs. We did not ... stealth is the key when it comes to submarines. If they are operated in close proximity, their distinctive under water and acoustic signatures, emissions can be made out." The Iranian navy has three kilo class vessels and the US is keen to measure the submarine's distinct underwater signatures. INS Viraat, India's only aircraft carrier, was also initially slated to take part in the exercises, but the plan was dropped.[20]

For three days from October 6, nearly 1500 personnel of the Indian and US navies and their battleships strode the waters, 70 to 200 nautical miles off the Malabar coast playing out fictional scenarios involving contraband control, anti-submarine maritime interdiction operations, air defence counter terrorism manoeuvres and sea control operations cross defence flying or landing helicopters on each other's deck for familiarization. Surface shoot, that is firing at a target by the ships surface guns; and UNREP (Replenishment, when the ships are underway) were also conducted jointly. The idea was to simulate a situation that might develop at sea and solve it. In the fifth exercise of its kind (in the Malabar series) anti-submarine operations were included for the first time. The VBSS (visit, board, search and seize) operations were also prectised to deal with probable threats of terrorism on the sea that loom large in the region. Those exercises were aimed at allowing the two navies to familiarize themselves with each other's philosophy and improve inter-operability. This seems natural as the two navies are dominant in the region.

In the words of Rear Admiral (Retd.) Sampath Gopal, "Joint exercises are important for any navy. The navies cannot be confined to any sea. We have to operate in international waters and to do that we have to know how other friendly navies operate. The joint exercises provide an opportunity for better navy-to-navy understanding. Each navy has its own operating philosophy. When two or three navies operate together it is very important to know not only the rules of the sea but also how others operate, inter-operability".[21]

For the enhanced naval cooperation 'DPG held its next meeting in August 6-7 2003 in Washington DC. the Undersecretary of Defence of policy, Douglas Faith, hosted the meeting and Defence undersecretary Ajay Prasad led the Indian delegation. Both sides agreed that the strategic situation in the world had changed dramatically. Global terrorism and state sponsorship of terrorism had increased and the proliferation of arms had become a key threat to international peace and security, and India and the United States had to come closer to deal with these new circumstances effectively.

Now the DPG emphasised the long-range strategic concepts that guide the new approach to the US- India relationship. They agreed on the work of the two countries together during the past year, and the planned activities for the next year are translating that strategic vision into action. Both the sides agreed to establish a high-level dialogue on defence technology security issues and reaffirmed the shared view that missile defence enhances cooperative security and stability. The two delegations also highlighted the importance of the ongoing series of joint and combined exercises in building interoperability between the United States and India and also agreed to continue this interaction.[22]

Joint Indo-US air, naval and special forces' counter-terrorism exercises in 2003, along with the resumption of DPG meetings mark a significant increase in security cooperation between the two countries.

Speaking at a Centre for Strategic and International Studies (CSIS) panel in Washington on "Bridging US-India: A Defence Perspective" three American observers of the US- Indo security relations agreed that a 'convergence of interests' is bringing the two nations towards closer ties. They also discussed as to how divergent expectations and perceptions of threat might impact the long-term strategic relationship.

In the opening remarks, the US Senate Foreign Relations Committee Chief Policy Advisor for South Asia Jonah Blank called China, Pakistan and counter-terrorism the three most important concerns driving US-Indian "Strategic Convergence of Interests". In separate remarks on the US-Indo Relations

(September 13, 2003 in New Delhi), the State Departments' Assistant secretary for South Asian Affairs, Christina Rocca, commented on the complementary objectives of the United States and India. She said, "In every instance, Indian and American objectives far from being antithetical are in fact complementary". She further said," India seeks a regional environment free of unrest, subversion and terrorism; the United States shares that objective. India seeks a regional environment where economic growth, trade and peaceful cross-national ties can prosper; The United States shares that objective too. India seeks a regional environment populated by liberal democratic states that are sensitive to diversity and the rights of minorities; the United States must certainly share that objective too".[23]

Despite such pronouncement the US actions are to the contrary. For example it doesn't feel comfortable in exporting /transferring technology to India which considers it very important to start believing in the American intentions. This was reflected in the words of Juli Macdonald when speaking at the same forum. This analyst at the Booz Allen Hamilton Consulting company said the US- India relationship is plagued by differing perceptions of threats and expectations. Based on interviews she conducted with over 80 defence officials and government policy-makers in both countries for a US Defence Department sponsored study ("The Indo-US Military relationship: Expectations and Perceptions," October 2002). She said, "Indian respondents desired a relationship built on equality", viewing technology transfer as the engine of the relationships. Many respondents, viewed the United States as an "unreliable partner, and "unreliable supplier of equipment".

According to this study, for the Indians technology transfer is the 'acid test' of US commitment, it demonstrates US confidence and trust in the relationship, it confirms the US understanding of India as a strategic partner and it signals that India is a friend and we treat India as a friend", Macdonald said,[24] Even if USA agrees to transfer technology, which seems highly inprobable and only a hypothetical possibility, there are other problems in a long-term relationship.

The essential dilemma of a regional power like India today is to what extent it can reconcile itself with the US power and presence in the region. It is true that the high-profile nature of the Indo-US naval exercises attract global attention and India is fast emerging as a force to reckon with in the Indian Ocean Region. Still there are no illusions left regarding the fire-power and agendas of these two navies. "Indian naval ships at best spend a week to a fortnight (not counting rare exceptions like INS Tarangini) on the high seas whereas the US navy ships spend months. Moreover the US ships can go to a number of friendly ports for spares and refits, rest and recuperation in addition to having a sound financial back-up. As far as the Indian navy is concerned, strategically and financially it is meant only to protect its own waters even though its 'vision' may be set far beyond its waters,[25] and it may be trying to become a 'blue water navy'.

Though Indo-US naval cooperation has grown at a rapid pace in the past few years, there have also been expressions of doubts and misgivings about it and not without a sound reasoning, such as;

1. **Issue of Terrorism**: Can both the countries really agree upon what constitutes terrorism and how to deal with it in different parts of the world?

2. **Democratic values in Asia:** Can both the countries have a common position on pluralism and human rights? Can they join together in condemning anti-democratic rules all over the world?

3. **India's' Regional Character:** Despite the eroded spirit of Afro-Asianism and non-alignment they cannot be ignored even today as India has had historic commitments with them, and even in the changed circumstances India is expected to stand up and speek out in favour of these lofty ideals even if it has to oppose the United States in doing so. Can India still play this role and together with it

maintain its newly formed close ties with the United States? Even when it is trying to find new vistas of co-operation with the United States and does find a new framework for cooperation with the United States in the Indian Ocean beyond the issue of Kashmir, can India really overcome all these hurdles and **'fight-together'** with the United States in the long run? It is difficult, if not impossible, despite the increasing and apparent bonhomie between the two countries. There have been notes of dissent in India on the growing Indo-US naval cooperation and specially about the joint naval exercises between the two. "Left parties have flayed these joint exercises terming them as 'detrimental to the security of the nation. The CPI (M) state secretary (Kerala) said that the Indo-US naval exercises would have far reaching repercussions on the country's security. According to him, the joint-naval exercises were unprecedented in scale and scope and indicated that India wished to have close links with the United States' armed forces. The war games, he said, would throw the door open for American imperialist forces to take advantage of India's vulnerabilities.

The CPI state secretary termed the exercises as a 'part of clear agenda to co-opt India to the Israel US axis'. Commenting on the development, he said, "The war games world result in India becoming yet another pawn in the hands of the imperialist forces. The US is using Israel as a weapon against the Palestinian people today. Tomorrow, it may use India against its future enemies, he said.

The RSP state secretary said, "the naval exercises would give the United States an opportunity to achieve its long-cherished hegemony in the Indian Waters." He further warned. "The Vajpayee governments decision to surrender the nations territorial waters to a foreign power run counter to all tenets of national security. Coming as it did at a time when India was faced with serious threats from Pakistan, the experience that the US navy had gained from the naval exercises could well prove beneficial to Pakistan."[26]

If these statements, which appear to be stretching the threat too far, are read and analysed in the light of two other news items, they project an entirely different picture altogether.

As early as on 28 April 1994 a news was published in *The Hindu* under the topic, 'US Navy wants permanent force in Indian Ocean. This news said, The US navy has called for a permanent carrier task force in the Indian Ocean", according to the US media.

The prospect for the permanent presence of the United States navy in this quarter has been conceived as a balance to the growing regional navies of India, China and Japan as well as a more effective measure for the dual containment of Iraq and Iran once the force is constituted. There would be at least four carriers foraging the Indian Ocean waters. According to the US navy's rule of Thumb, it takes four carriers to keep: one station- one in transit, one on home leave, one in repair and one on duty. The proposed task force would see a US carrier in the ocean.[27]

If this appears an exaggeration there was another news article in *Outlook* which detailed spying in the Indian waters, without any reason despite the ongoing joint exercises between India and the United States. Most part of this article is reproduced here to prove the point, and for ready reference.[28]

This must be the first case of serious organised spying on the Indian navy to come to light in the last decade. Last month, navy headquarters dashed off a detailed note to the Ministry of defence (MoD) raising serious objections to an American warship spying consistently for several months in 2002-2003 and carrying out unauthorised exercise off the Visakhapatnam coast well inside India's exclusive economic zone (EEZ). The area under survey was too close for comfort to the strategic naval base at Visakhapatnam. The spying operations were conducted under the garb of 'research' and without prior permission, flouting all rules of engagement. Such 'intrusions', say senior naval officers, could well lead to a compromising of India's security.

The detailed note from the naval headquarters to the MoD (accessed by *Outlook*) raised serious concern about the presence of the American warship USS Bowditch in India's EEZ. The warship, ostensibly granted rights to conduct 'survey and research', seems to have exceeded its brief and there is a clear suggestion that it was spying to assess India's hidden naval capabilities. "The navy", say a senior naval officer, "regards this American act as illegal, against international rule and without the permission of the Indian government."

In the note, the naval headquarters has said that the American warship had clearly violated Indian and International law. "Notwithstanding the US position... the so-called military survey and research is a facade or smokescreen to camouflage their actual intent," it points out. The navy has also proposed that the ministry take up the issue "strongly through diplomatic channels, failing which the matter be referred to relevant bodies in the United Nations as an international dispute."

The note outlines a number of issues. The USS Bowditch carried out an ocean military surveillance within the EEZ comprising 250 nautical miles of Indian territory. The navy says the warship gathered data that could reveal much military information on the ocean environment, including identifying possible underground nuclear facilities and submarines. Such data helps reorient technology in undersea warfare and enemy ship detection.

According to the navy, the ship, in direct contravention of well-laid down international laws, mapped the ocean floor, carried out seabed studies, including topography, nature and type of sediments, acoustic signal range limitation observations, assessed temperature, salinity, sound velocity and sea current profiles using state-of-the-art sensors. "It is clear from the above that the type of activities the vessel is capable of carrying out include various kinds of acoustic surveys.' Measurements of parameters is prohibited under existing guidelines on the subject by the ministry of defence," the navy wrote in its note.

According to Naval HQ, the US ship deliberately violated the Law of Sea convention of 1982. "Those wishing to undertake research in another state's EEZ are subject to various regulations. First it must provide the coastal state (in this case India) with specific information about the proposed project at least six months in advance. Second, it must allow the coastal state to participate or be represented in the project. Thirdly, it must provide the coastal state with the results of the research. Failure to comply with these obligations entitles the coastal state to suspend the research or require its cessation," the note stated. The USS Bowditch did nothing of the kind and quietly left the Indian shores some time in late 2003.

Adds Admiral Raja Menon (retd): a "very delicate situation, even though such an incident did occur once in the early 90s, the Americans do not want their freedom of the seas to be curtailed in any way. The best way out of this would be that the information be shared between two maritime powers, India and the US." The navy has challenged the US interpretation of events. The US contention that the military survey activities are related to freedom of navigation on the high seas and they can carry out such activities in the EEZ of the coastal state is wrong interpretation of relevant laws.... Freedom of navigation does not give absolute right to a warship to carry out resource-oriented research without the consent of the coastal state," says the note. It also adds that "The concept of military survey activities coined by the US is not available under any laws of sea governing the international community. Such activities under the garb of 'high seas', freedom or freedom of navigation are also not permissible under UN laws." Says former navy chief Admiral. R.H. Tahiliani, "The charges are serious. The navy knows what it's saying. It can't be a frivolous complaint." Agrees Col. P.N. Kneer, editor, Asian Defence News International: "under the garb of joint Indo-US defence cooperation, no unauthorised intrusion should be allowed. The Indian protest should be strong and vigorous."

Interestingly, the same vessel was misused for spying purposes and was intercepted inside its EEZ by the Chinese navy in March 2001 and forced to turn back at gunpoint. Naval researches studying similar US research requests to different countries between 1972 and 1978 says that a majority of them were rejected outright and in those cases where permission was granted, the surveys were conducted under strict surveillance of the coastal country concerned. In 1968, North Korea found another US warship, Pueblo, allegedly spying in its EEZ under the guise of a research vessel. Since then many countries have been wary of entertaining such requests from the US navy. India doesn't seem to have learnt its lessons from other countries' experiences.

Both nations and both navies have long memories. Much will depend on the regard shown to each other's sensitivities. There are not many scholars in the US who are sufficiently acquainted with the Indian navy. Nor are there many scholars who have grasped the historical and contemporary compulsions that drive the US navy, the number of well informed scholars on both sides will also increase gradually in step with the frequency and intensity of Indo-US strategic and Indo-US naval interaction. Meanwhile the events after 9/11 augur well as well so we should not expect too much from each other.

References

1. Sri Latha, V. "Indo-US naval cooperation in the Indian Ocean", Indian Ocean Digest, Vol. 17, No. 2, July-Dec. 2002 pp. 22-29.
2. ... from the sea, at http://www.militaryinfo.com
3. *Ibid*.
4. Summer, G. Harry Jr. "Are US forces over-stretched: Operations, Procurement and Industrial Base," Strategic Digest, Vol. 27, No. 6, June 1997, p. 824.
5. "Forward from the sea' at http://www.militaryinfo.com
6. *Ibid*, "Navy Operational Concept".
7. "Operational Fleet to Run US Navy Experience, Strategic Digest, Vol.32, No. 11, November 2002.
8. Singh, Ravi Pratap, "Rogue Doctrine and Missile Defence. A Prescription for more Aggression, more Intervention," India Quarterly, Vol. 57. No. 3, July Sep. 2001.

9. Rao, P.V., "Indian Ocean and the Pax Americana", Indian Ocean Digest, Vol. 17, No. 1, January-June 2002, p. 1-16.
10. *Ibid.*
11. Sakhuja, Vijay, "Indo-US Naval cooperation", Institute of Peace and Conflict Studies, Article 898, Oct. 2002
12. *Ibid.*
13. *Ibid.*
14. Unnithan, Sandeep, "Close Encounters", India Today, October 20, 2003, pp. 66-67.
15. Sakhuja, Vijay *op.cit.*
16. Unnitan, Sandeep, *op. cit.*
17. Sri Latha, V., *op. cit.*
18. Sharma, Ravi, "On Board INS Brahmputra and USS Chosin", Vol. 20, Issue 22. http://www.flonnet.com/fl.2022/stories/2003/1107002504200 .htm
19. Unnithan, Sandeep, *op. cit.*
20. Sharma, Ravi, *op. cit.*
21. *Ibid.*
22. "What is hot?" Analysis of Recent Happenings, Indo-US DPG-Joint Statement, An IDC Analysis, 11.8.2003 http://www.indiadefence.com/ DPG-joint.htm.
23. Kujawa, Anthony, "Convergence of Interests Leading to Closer Indo-US Security Ties", press release -US Consulate Chennai, 15 Dec.2003.
24. *Ibid.*
25. *Ibid.*
26. Nair, Gouridasan, "Indo-US-Naval Exercise Poses Security Threat", The Hindu, 8.10.2003.
27. 'US Navy Wanted Permanent-Force in Indian Ocean", The Hindu, 28.4.1994.
28. Bhushan, Ranjit, "Port Hole", Outlook, June 7, 2004, pp 16-18.

9

Conclusions

"The only thing necessary for the triumph of evil is for a good man to do nothing". How true these words are of Edmund Burke! Especially in the world of today when the entire human culture and civilization is threatened by acts of terrorism and other similar menaces. Similar trends that threaten human security are aided by the ever growing militarization and nuclearization of the world. Now we possess weapons of mass destruction that can annihilate the whole human civilization not once but many times over.

This shows that we have lost the 'sense of direction' and when one loses the sense of direction or reason these words of the Roman writer *Seneca* turn to be true, **"If a man does not know to what port he is steering, no wind is favourable."** These are echoed in the words of the German philosopher Nietzsehe, **"Man's most enduring stupidity is forgetting what he is trying to do"**. Here the question arises: are we progressing on the path of self-destruction by not knowing what we are doing and where we are heading to? By not listening to the calls of reason and by not knowing what the result of our actions is going to be are we in our sheer innocence or stupidity progressing in the direction from where it would become impossible to retrace our steps? Are we in our greed and haste for development, exploiting natural resources, land and marine, in a manner that will leave nothing for our future generations? Are we causing irreparable damage to our environment and unimaginable damage to our future?

No, no human race as a whole can be so stupid and ignorant. True, there are fanatics, fundamentalists and terrorists; there are people 'in a hurry' and governments led by the people who are short-sighted and cannot think beyond their petty interests or immediate future. There are always people and governments who have no vision, do not listen to the voice of sanity and even suppress their conscience. But, there are others too and human kind is fortunate in having them, who know exactly what they are doing, what they should be doing and have a 'vision'. These people listen to the calls of reason and sanity and call upon us all to follow the path of trust instead of suspicion, of cooperation rather than of confrontation and of peace, and development instead of war and destruction. In the hands of such people only the future of human civilization can be safe and secure.

We need to listen to such people in the Indian Ocean Region. This is imperative looking at the forever present and growing instances of political instability, confrontation and a state of flux that the region has been a host to. These trends pose a threat to the peace in the region and can turn into a reality at any time on the slightest pretext. Though there are many countries recognised as Indian Ocean countries and many extra-regional countries that have high stakes in this region, India and the United States play a big role in the region. India being the largest kid on the bloc and the USA being the only superpower in a multi-polar world can play an effective peace-keeping role by adopting and implementing policies of peace and cooperation. The relations between these two countries without any doubt will influence the events in this region as well as the prospects of establishing and sustaining peace. Of course these two will have to be helped by other like-minded countries in the region without which the efforts to establish peace can never bear fruit.

I

War, Commerce and Piracy are and have always been **the three vital factors at sea**. The Indian Ocean, the third largest Ocean of the world on which the destiny of the **world is to be decided**[1] in this century has always had all the three.

Commercially, it is the most important sea through which the major sea lines of communication pass carrying a large portion of the entire world trade. Piracy has once again become rampant on these waters specially, in South China Sea. There is always a probability of war in the surrounding region as the region is politically unstable, lacks cooperation, is surrounded by major religions i.e. Islam, Hinduism and Christianity among which **'a Clash'**[2] at any time cannot be ruled out. The region is a kaleidoscope of isms as well-socialism, communism, fundamentalism, feudalism, tribalism, adventurism and yes, terrorism too with a spectrum of political hues ranging from democracy, monarchy to military dictatorships. A clash among different ideologies would also not be unimaginary.

Looking at the growing importance of the oceans the United Nations had declared 1998 as **'The Year of the Oceans**; this emphasised the fact that the neglect of ocean environment will imperil mankind's ability to use the sea in all other ways as, **'if this goes everything goes'**. Today when the world is going through and progressing towards globalization and the whole wide world has turned into 'a village', the resultant impact is **"Death of Distance"**. With the elimination of distance the high seas have also shrunk. This shrinking of the high seas is not just in a lateral way with the extension of the territorial seas but metamorphically too, because the process of globalization meant that geographical distance matters so much less than it did.

This has helped in a better realization of the relevance and importance of the seas in general. 'Proximity' of interests is that matters. Earlier the general public was not educated about the water as it is about the land because, the seas were distant and not expected to have any impact on their day-to-day lives. Governments also didn't pay enough attention to their surrounding waters. With the expansion of information technology the picture has changed now. Recent marine research showing the importance and impact of marine environment on human life has been reaching the general public making them sensitive to the issues pertaining to the oceans. This is helped by the ever-growing scarcity of drinking water on the land, lack of food grains and dwindling metals and minerals in reverse proportion of their growing dependence by the increasing human population.

Now, after nearly exhausting the land resources, the marine resources are being the centre of attraction to people and governments. They are looking forward to the oceans as having a solution to all their problems. They expect to have enough potable water through the process of reverse osmosis, depend more and more on fish and other sea food and are hoping to fulfil the needs of oil and energy for their industries by exploiting the sea beds more economically. The realization of the economic worth of the seas has enhanced their importance in the human eye (but can also forecast doom) for their future. Human beings have mercilessly exploited the land resources without taking care to replenish them and now they may do the same to the marine resources. An increasing awareness regarding the economic worth of the marine resources can lead to wars as did the land resources. Hence the need to establish and maintain peace has increased manifold in the past few years.

Now everyone has an increasing interest in what happens 'over there' and in consequence the intervening ocean areas are better seen as joining distant countries rather than separating them, giving credence to the Norwegian saying, "**Land divides but the sea Unites**. With the increasing importance of the oceans, the whole maritime world, navies included, is going through a period and a process of particularly accelerated change. We have indeed come a long way from 1609 when Hugo Grotius had first stated the doctrine of **"freedom of the seas"**. In his words, **"the ocean which rather possesses the earth rather than is by it possessed... cannot become private property"**. The oceans even today are seen as, "Common heritage of mankind". Though this principle is limited to the high seas only which have considerably shrunk from the times of Hugo Grotius and are expected to shrink further as people and nations start claiming more and more nautical miles as their own.

This has led to discussions, deliberations and codification of international sea law, which is a very important part of international law today. Here it would be appropriate to look into certain changes in the sea law affected by the 1982 convention.

II

The third United Nations convention on the law of the sea (The 1982 Convention) came into force on 16 November 1994. An overwhelming number of states (157) had put their signatures on this convention[3] the very first day it was open for signatures in December 1982. 142 states plus the European Union have since ratified this convention. Still, there are 30 coastal states (including some signatories) and 26 landlocked countries that have not ratified or acceded to this convention. Here it is worth mentioning that though the United States has contributed much to strengthen the unified application of the convention, it has still not signed or acceded to the convention, despitethe the best efforts by the parties concerned (some changes were introduced to the sea-bed regime by the 1994 New York Implementation Agreement to remove the United States' difficulties with the convention).

Geographical Scene - A decision in early 2000 by the International Hydrographic Organization to delimit the oceans has shrunk the area of the Indian Ocean. The revised surface area of the Indian Ocean is about 68,650 million square kilometres (still the third largest ocean after the Pacific and the Atlantic). The Indian Ocean includes the,

1. Andaman Sea
2. Arabian Sea
3. Arafura Sea
4. Bay of Bengal
5. Great Australian Bight
6. Gulf of Aden
7. Gulf of Oman

8. Mozambique channel
9. Persian Gulf
10. Red Sea
11. Timor Sea, and
12. The straits of Malacca and Singapore and other interconnecting water bodies.

Its main choke points are,

1. Bab-al-Mandeb
2. Strait of Hormuz
3. Straits of Malacca and Singapore
4. Southern access to the Suez canal, and
5. The Lombok and Sunda straits.

The great importance of the Indian Ocean is dependent on the fact that it not only provides the major sea-routes connecting the Middle East, Africa and East Asia with Europe and America which carry the heavy traffic of petroleum and petroleum products to energy hungry economies, it is also rich in both the living and non-living resources which makes it very attractive for extra regional powers. Terrorism, piracy, political instability, weak economies, lack of any strong regional forum (including the SAARC and IOR-ARC), demand for greater regional autonomy in some countries of the region and the recognition of indigenous rights to territory and resources-on-shore and off-shore, establishment of naval bases by some countries in the region, environmental pollution, threats to human security are major geopolitical and economic issues faced by the region. Of these the environment has gained so much importance and concerns and awareness regarding pollution of environment and the disastrous impact of the same is raised so high that they are now reflected by a new term Geo-Economic Environment (GEE).

Maritime Jurisdiction - In the past few years a lot has been achieved and still is being done in the sphere of maritime jurisdiction and codification of international sea law. Some of the issues in this regard need special mention here to highlight the importance of the oceans and their resources in the coming times.

The 1982 convention recognizes five additional jurisdictional zones in addition to internal waters, the territorial waters and the contiguous zone. These are,

1. The Continental Shelf
2. The Exclusive Economic Zone
3. The Exclusive Fishing Zone
4. Archipelagic Waters ,and
5. The High Seas and The Area.

The first four are generally discussed at length in all academic discussions but for the purposes of this study the high seas and the area are for more important.

The high seas are that part of the sea which is not claimed or included in the littoral waters, territorial sea, EEZ of a state or in the archipelagic waters of an archipelagic state. The high seas as is evident from the very name are open to all states and should be used for peaceful purposes only. Five freedoms of the high seas are:

1. Freedom of navigation.
2. Freedom of laying submarine cables and pipelines.
3. Freedom of construction of artificial islands and other installations.
4. Freedom of fishing, and
5. Freedom of carrying out scientific research.

Beneath the high seas is 'The Area' defined by the convention as 'the seabed and Ocean floor, the sub-soil thereof beyond the limits of the national jurisdiction (which) as well as the resources of The Area remain the **Common heritage of mankind**. No state may claim or exercise sovereignty or sovereign rights over any part of The Area or its resources.

"The Common Heritage of Mankind", the principle that is generally misunderstood was passed by the United Nations General Assembly by a vote of 106 to 0 in 1970. At that time the United States had voted in favour of the principle and only the Soviet block had abstained.

Central to the common heritage was the principle that the profits were to be distributed to all the countries of the world in inverse relation to their dues to the United Nations. This meant that, although all countries would eventually benefit from the common heritage, the poorer countries would benefit proportionally more than the rich. At that time the principle was not opposed by many and had general acceptance. However, the Regan administration that had come to power in the United States didn't favour the principle of 'common heritage' and it is still pending before the US senate, waiting to receive its **"advise and consent"**.

III

Briton Sir Julian Corbett, American Alfred Thayer Mahan, Indian Scholars like K. M. Pannikkar and K.B. Vaidya, like many others emphasised in their wrilings upon thc importance of the oceans, navies and other aspects related to these two. Since then the importance and worth of the oceans has increased manifold in all three aspects, geo-strategic, economic and environmental. Hence, the renewed interest in these subjects. Still enough attention is not being paid to the oceans by the general *public*, which remains blissfully unaware and ignorant of the threats looming large. Hence I would like to mention only three such threats, though others are by no means less important. These three threats are:

1. Piracy
2. Terrorism, and
3. Pollution of marine environment

When one mentions piracy the general reaction is - aren't you talking about pirated books and software? Sea Pirates!

Of course there are no sea pirates now. They were a phenomenon of bygone era. They now exist in fiction only. Well, nothing can be more far from the truth. Piracy has returned with a bang, especially in areas like South China Sea. It is once again threatening the freedom of navigation on the seas in addition to causing grave financial losses to merchant shipping, not to mention the threat of closing down of important sea-lanes. Willingly or unwillingly by the acts of pirates important sea-lanes can be closed down for indefinite periods. This may result in the closing down of SLOC's which may in turn put heavy demands on the industries and economies of all energy hungry countries that depend on the import of oil.

Terrorism! Well we are all aware and much concerned about terrorism and terrorists after the events of the 9/11. Still least attention is paid to maritime terrorism or terrorism on the high seas. At best people laugh it away as something 'impossible'. They generally do not find any sense in even discussing its possibility. But, did any one predict the possibility of 9/11 attacks? And then certain acts of pirates (e.g. attacks on M.V. Limburg and USS Cole) can conveniently be classified as acts of terrorists. If we do not pay any attention to this form of terrorism now, we may have to repent later and much more than we did after 9/11. The terrorism on the high seas can be much more dangerous and devastating in all its aspects/forms than the terrorism on the land.

Acts of pirates and terrorists can also cause havoc to human security, directly or indirectly. As a result of such acts even the marine environment is threatened. Due to oil spills and release of nuclear material irreparable damage can be caused. Such disasters are much more difficult to manage on the water than the sea because of the many factors involved in such events.

All these threats have increased the importance of the oceans and navies for all the countries concerned whether they have direct or indirect involvement. Now the need is to sensitise the masses about these matters. One positive outcome of such developments is that now the countries have realized the importance of cooperation (naval) to deal with such threats. That is why nowadays we witness the increased importance given to the navies the world over and their expanding role. This has also resulted in more and more joint naval exercises among almost all the sea-faring nations than were ever witnessed in the past. Take the example of the Indo-US, Indo-French, Indo-China, and Indo-South East Asian Nation's joint naval exercises. Such trends would help the countries of the world or at least their navies to come closer even if their respective governments keep grappling with other unsolved problems.

IV

Though the regional as well as the extra regional countries realize that they have to make their presence felt on the oceans, specially in the Indian Ocean to protect and promote their national interests, they also realize that they have to cooperate with each other to achieve their aims. In today's trends of globalization, liberalization and interdependence they could not expect to go solo all the way notwithstanding their economic or military power. The Indian Ocean countries are no exception to this realization; hence they had established IOR-ARC for enhancing cooperation among themselves in addition to similar forums at the regional level e.g. ASEAN, SAARC and APEC. The need of the hour is to make such organizations stronger and build confidence-building measures (CBM's) to enhance trust and cooperation in place of suspicions and confrontations. This can be achieved only when forced by the circumstances these countries will have to keep their eyes open and realize their limitations of spending their dear and scarce resources on maintaining maritime security. For example, the USA did the same to save time and money and as a result held **'operation enduring freedom'** in collaboration with India. In this endeavor both Indian and American naval ships escorted their merchant ships carrying high risk materials through the pirate infested Malacca straits on a six month basis.

To enhance naval cooperation and peace steps can be taken in the following areas:

1. Exchange of naval visits and conduct of more joint naval exercises to increase inter-operatibility
2. Greater transparency by setting up a regional ship plot and by providing advance information about naval exercises as is done in the case of military exercises.
3. Setting up of joint task forces to respond to natural calamities such as cyclones, famines and SAR operations (Search and Rescue) at sea.
4. Joint efforts to tackle/ control maritime pollution, for the conservation of marine environment, combat drug trafficking, smuggling, terrorism, piracy, etc.
5. Fish know no boundaries so do fishermen; more often than not this creates problems among the nations regarding their exclusive economic and fishing zones. Fisherman who are arrested on charges of violations of these boundaries should be dealt with more leniently to avoid the flaring up of other political problems between the sovereign states.
6. Strong regional organizations should be established that have the task of looking into ecological, economic and political problems in this order. To emphasise upon these aspects a new word is coined 'eco-eco- development' (ecological and economic development).
7. More countries should establish 'Maritime Universities' to enhance scientific research as well as create awareness in the general public.
8. Countries should decide not to deploy nuclear weapons on the waters (though it is very tempting and hence very difficult to achieve).

There can be no dispute on the need to establish peace in the Indian Ocean Region. The only way to proceed towards achieving this cherished goal is through establishing trust, confidence and cooperation among the people and nations that are so very different in culture, religion, political belief and economic and military status. Long lasting hostilities and natural suspicion make the process very difficult and frustratingly slow; still this appears to be the only way towards peace and cooperation. All have a role to play in this process, nations of east and west, developed and developing, maritime and landlocked, littoral and hinterland, big and small and it would be due to the efforts of all concerned that humankind may proceed towards safety, peace and development instead of destruction, devastation and ultimate annihilation. The choice is with us all and the time to act is now.

REFERENCES

1. Mahan, Alfred Thayer "The Influence of Sea Power upon History 1660-1783", Hill and Wang, New York, 1957.
2. Huntington, Samuel P. "The Clash of Civilization and The Remaking of World Order", Penguin, New Delhi, 1996.
3. Jose, Luis Jesus. "The Ocean's Wealth is Not Inexhaustible", UN Chronicle, No. 4, 2002.
4. John, Temple Swing, "What Future for the Oceans?, Foreign Affairs, Vol. 82 No. 5, Sept. - Oct. 2003; pp. 139-152.

Appendix A

Proposed geographic definition of the Indian ocean

1. The dividing line between the Atlantic and Indian Ocean is the meridian of Cape Agulhas (20° O′ E).
2. The dividing line between the Pacific and Indian Ocean is the meridian of the south-east cape of Tasmania (147° O′ E), the Western exit of the Bass Strait and the median line between the north-west of Australia and the Malay peninsula (Cape Talbot through Timor, Sumba, Flores and the Sunda Islands, up to Sumatra).
3. The dividing line between the Atlantic Ocean and the Indian Ocean is the (60° O′ E).
4. The northern limits of the Indian Ocean are clearly defined.

   Source: Un Document A/AC. 159/1, July 1974

Appendix B

Statistical data on the Indian ocean region countries

	Area (Km^2)	Capital	Form of Government
1. The South East			
Australia	7,678,000	Canberra	parl. democracy
Burma	677,000	Rangoon	republic
Indonesia	1,904,000	Jakarta	republic
Malaysia	330,000	Kuala Lumpur	elected monarchy
Thailand	514,000	Bangkok	kingdom
2. South Asia			
Afghanistan	647,000	Kabul	republic
Bangladesh	144,000	Dhaka	republic
Bhutan	47,000	Thimpu	kingdom
India	3,288,000	New Delhi	republic
Maldives	298	Male	republic
Nepal	141,000	Kathmandu	kingdom
Pakistan	892,000	Islamabad	republic
Sri Lanka	66,000	Colombo	republic
3. The Persian Gulf			
Bahrain	622	Manama	sheikhdom
Iran	1,684,000	Tehran	republic
Qatar	11,000	Doha	sheikhdom
Kuwait	18,000	Kuwait	sheikhdom
Oman	212,000	Muscat	sultanate

	Area (Km^2)	Capital	Form of Government
Saudi Arabia	2,150,000	Riyadh	kingdom
United Arab Emirates	84,000	Abu Dhabi	federation of sheikhdom
4. The horn of Africa and the Red Sea			
Egypt	1,000,000	Cairo	republic
Ethiopia	1,222,000	Addis Ababa	republic
Djibouti	22,000	Djibouti	republic
Israel	21,000	Jerusalem	republic
Jordan	98,000	Amman	kingdom
Somalia	638,000	Mogadishu	republic
Sudan	2,506,000	Khartoum	republic
North Yemen	195,000	Sanaa	republic
South Yemen	333,000	Aden	republic
5. Eastern and Southern Africa			
Botswana	600,000	Gaberone	republic
Kenya	583,000	Nairobi	republic
Lesotho	30,000	Maseru	kingdom
Malawi	118,000	Lilongwe	republic
Mozambique	783,000	Maputo	republic
Zambia	753,000	Lusaka	republic
Swaziland	17,000	Mbabane	kingdom
Zimbabwe	391,000	Harare	republic
South Africa	1,221,000	Pretoria	republic
6. Island States in the Western Indian Ocean			
Comoros	2,171	Moroni	republic
Madagascar	587,000	Tananarive	republic
Mauritius	2,045	Port Louis	republic
Seychelles	278	Victoria	republic

Source: IISS, The Military Balance, 1980/81, London 1980.

Appendix - C

Coastline measurement of the Indian ocean littoral states

Country (Political Division)	Capital	Nautical miles
1. Australia (continent)	Canberra	13.971
2. Indonesia (13,500 island)	Jakarta	19,889
3. Portuguese Timor		33
4. Singapore	Singapore	28
5. Malaysia (MalaysWest Coast)	Kuala Lumpur	440
6. Thailand (West coast on Andaman sea)	Bangkok	324
7. Burma	Rangoon	1,230
8. Bangladesh	Dhaka	230
9. India	New Delhi	2,759
10. Sri Lanka (Ceylon)	Colombo	650
11. Maldive Islands	Male	Not available
12. Pakistan	Islamabad	440
13. Iran	Tehran	990
14. Iraq	Baghdad	10
15. Kuwait	Kuwait	115
16. Saudi Arabia (on Persian Gulf)	Riyadh	296
17. Bahrain	Manama	68
18. Qatar	Doha	204

Country (Political Division)	Capital	Nautical miles
19. United Arab Emirates	Abu Dhabi	420
20. Oman	Muscat	1,005
21. Peoples Republic of Yemen	Aden	654
22. Arab Republic of Yemen	Sanaa	244
23. Saudi Arabia (on Red Sea)	-	1020
24. Jordan	Amman	5
25. Israel (on Gulf of Aqaba)	Jerusalem	4
26. Egypt (on Red Sea)	Cairo	769
27. Sudan	Khasfoum	387
28. Ethiopia	Addis Ababa	546
29. French territory of Afans and Issas	Djibouti	123
30. Somalia	Mogadishu	1,596
31. Kenya	Nairobi	247
32. Tanzania (Including Zanzibar)	Dar-es-saleem	669
33. Mozambique	Lourenco Maruqes	1,352
34. Malagasy Republic (Madagascar)	Tananarive	2,155
35. Mauritius	Port Louis	87
36. Reunion	St. Denis	100
37. South Africa	Pretoria (administrative) Cape town (legislative)	1,430

1. The states are listed Counterclockwise
2. Indian Ocean Coastline about two-third, of this

Source: United States, Department of States, Sovereignty of the sea (Washington D.C.: Bureau of Intelligence and Research, 1965). Cited in Ference A. Vali, Politics of the Indian Ocean Region; The Balances of Power, The Free Press, New York, 1976, pp. 263-264.

Appendix D

Principal straits and channels in the Indian ocean region

Strait or channel	Geographic location	Width of narrowest section (Nautical Miles)
1. Bass strait	Between the Australia Continent and Tasmania	80
2. Torres Strait	Between Australia and New Guinea (Papua)	100
3. Wetal Strait	Between Portuguese Timor and Water Island (Indonesia)	50
4. Ombai Strait	Between Portuguese Timor and Alos Island (Indonesia)	16
5. Sape Strait	Between Komodo and Sumbawa Island (Indonesia)	8
6. Alas Strait	Between Lombok and Sumbawas Island (Indonesia)	5
7. Lombok Strait	Between Bali and Lombok Island (Indonesia)	11
8. Bali Strait	Between Bali and Java Island (Indonesia)	2

Strait or channel	Geographic location	Width of narrowest section (Nautical Miles)
9. Sunda Strait	Between Java and Sumatra (Indonesia)	12
10. Singapore Strait	Between Singapore and the Ria Islands (Indonesia)	8
11. Malacca Strait	Between Malaysia and Indonesia (Sumatra)	20
12. Palk Strait	Between India and Sri Lanka (Ceylon)	3
13. Hormuz Strait	Between Iran and Oman (Musandan Penins)	21
14. Bab el Mandeb	Between South Yemen and the French Territory of Afars and Issas	14
15. Tiran Strait	Between the Sinai Peninsula (Egypt	and Israeli occupies) and Saudi Arabia'
16. Zanzibar Channel	Between Zanzibar and the Tanzanian Main land	16
17. Mozambique Channel	Between Mozambique and Madagascar (Malagasy Republic)	250

The strait and channel are listed counterclockwise.

Source : United States, Department of State, Sovereignty of the Sea (Washington D.C.: Bureau of Intelligence and Research 1965); and United Nations, A Brief Geographical and Hydrographical study of straits (by Commander R.H. Kennedy), Document A/Conf.13/6 and Add. 1,1957. cited in Ference A. Vali *op. cit.*

Appendix E

UN resolution on a zone of peace, December 1971

General Assembly - Subject: Declaration of the Indian Ocean as a Zone of Peace. Resolution 2832 (XXVI), 16 December 1971.

The General Assembly

Conscious of the determination of the peoples of the littoral and hinterland States of the Indian Ocean to preserve that independence, sovereignty and territorial integrity, and to resolve their political, economic and social problems under conditions of peace and tranquillity,

Recalling the Declaration of the Third Conference of Heads of State or Government of Non-Aligned Countries, held at Lusaka in September 1970, calling up all States to consider and respect the Indian Ocean as a zone of peace from which great power rivalries and competition as well as bases conceived in the context of such rivalries and competition should be excluded, and declaring that the area should also be free to exclude, and convinced of the desirability of ensuring the maintenance of such conditions in the area by man's other obligations that call for the diversion of the limited resources of these States from more compelling and productive task of economic and social reconstruction and could further involve them in the rivalries of power blocks in a manner prejudicial to their independence and freedom of action, thereby increasing international tensions, Concerned at recent development that portend the extension of the arms race into the Indian ocean area, thereby posing a serious threat to the maintenance of such conditions in the area, Convinced that the establishment of a zone of peace in the Indian Ocean would contribute towards arresting such developments, relaxing international tensions and strengthening international peace and security,

Convinced further that the establishment of a zone of peace in an extensive geographical area in one region could have a beneficial influence on the establishment of permanent universal peace based on equal rights and justice for all, in accordance with the purpose and principles of the Charter of the United Nations,

1. Solemnly declares that the Indian Ocean, within limits to be determined, together with the air space above and the ocean floor subjacent thereto, is hereby designated for all times as a zone of peace;
2. Calls upto the great Powers, in conformity with the Declaration, to enter into immediate consultations with the littoral States of the Indian Ocean with a view to :
    (a) Halting the further escalation and expansion of their military presence in the Indian Ocean;
    (b) Eliminating from the Indian Ocean all bases, military installations, logistical supply facilities, the disposition of nuclear weapons and weapons of mass destruction and any manifestation of great power military presence in the Indian Ocean conceived in the context of great Power rivalry;
3. Calls upon the littoral and hinterland States of the Indian Ocean, the permanent member of the Security Council and other major maritime users of the Indian Ocean, in pursuit of the objective of establishing a system of universal collective security without military alliances and strengthening international security through regional and other co-operation, to enter into consultations with a view to the implementation of this Declaration and such action as may be necessary to ensure that :

(a) Warships and military aircraft may not use the Indian Ocean for any threat or use of force against the sovereignty, territorial integrity or independence of any littoral or hinterland States of the Indian Ocean in contravention of the purpose and principles of the Charter of the United Nations;

(b) Subject to the foregoing and to the norms and principles of international law, the right to free and unimpeded use of the zone by the vessels of all nations is unaffected;

(c) Appropriate arrangements are made to give effect to any international law, the right to free and unimpeded use of the zone by the vessels of all nations is unaffected;

4. Requests the secretary-general to report to the General Assembly at its twenty-seventh session on the progress that has been made with regard to the implementation of the Declaration;

5. Decide to include the item Entitled "Declaration of the Indian Ocean as a zone of peace" in the provisional agenda of its twenty-seventh session.

Recorded vote

In favour of: Afghanistan, Algeria, Bhutan, Burma, Burundi, Cameroon, Ceylon, Chad, China, Colombia, Congo, Costa Rica, Cyprus, Egypt, El Salvador, Equatorial Guinea, Ethiopia, Ghana, Guinea, Guyana, Island, India, Indonesia, Iran, Japan, Jordan, Kenya, Khmer Republic, Kuwait, Laos, Lebanon, Liberia, Libya, Malaysia, Mali, Malta, Mauritania, Mexico, Morocco, Nepal,

[1]Nicaragua, Nigeria, Pakistan, Panama, Qatar, Romania, Saudi Arabia, Somalia, Sudan, Swaziland, Sweden, Syria, Togo, Trinidad and Tobago, Tunisia, Uganda, United Republic of Tanzania, Uruguay, Yemen, Yugoslavia, Zambia.

1. Later advised the secretariat it had intended to abstain.

Against: None.

Abstaining: Argentina, Australia, Austria, Belgium, Bolivia, Brazil, Bulgaria, Byelorussia, Canada, Central Africa Republic, Chile, Cuba, Czechoslovakia, Dahomey, Denmark, Dominican Republic, Fiji, Finland, France, Greece, Guatemala, Haiti, Honduras, Hungary, Ireland, Israel, Italy, Ivory Coast, Jamaica, Lesotho, Luxembourg, Madagascar, Mongolia, Netherlands, New Zealand, Norway, People's Democratic Republic of Yemen, Peru, Philippines, Poland, Portugal, Rwanda, Senegal, Singapore, South Africa, Spain, Thailand, Turkey, Ukraine, USSAR, United Kingdom, United States, Upper Volta, Venezuela Zaire.

Absent: Albania, Bahrain, Barbados, Botswana, Ecuador, Gabon, Gambia,[1]Iraq, Malawi, Maldives, Mauritius, Niger, Oman, Paraguay, Sierra Leone, United Arab Emirates.

1. Later advised the secretariat it had intended to vote in favour

Appendix F

Charter of the Indian Ocean Rim Association for Regional Cooperation (IOR-ARC)

1. Conscious of historical bonds created through millennia among peoples of the Indian Ocean and with a sense of recovery of history; cognizant of economic transformation and speed of change the world over which is propelled significantly by increased intensity in regional economic cooperation; realising that the countries washed by the Indian Ocean in their diversity offer vast opportunities to enhance economic interaction and cooperation over a wide spectrum to mutual benefit and in a spirit of equality; convinced that the Indian Ocean Rim, by virtue of past shared experience and geo-economic linkages among Member States, is poised for the creation of an effective association and practical modalities of economic cooperation; and conscious of their responsibility to promote the welfare of their peoples by improving their standards of living and quality of life; the Governments of Australia, India, Indonesia, Kenya, Madagascar, Malaysia, Mauritius, Mozambique, Oman, Singapore, South Africa, Sri Lanka, Tanzania, Yemen hereby establish the Indian Ocean Rim Association for Regional Cooperation (IOR-ARC), with the following fundamental principles, objectives, areas of cooperation, and institutional and financial structures and arrangements.

Fundamental Principles

2. The Association will facilitate and promote economic cooperation, bringing together representatives of

government, business and academia. In a spirit of multilateralism, the Association seeks to build and expand understanding and mutually beneficial cooperation through a consensus-based, evolutionary and non-intrusive approach. The Association will apply the following fundamental principles without qualification or exception to all Member States:

(i) Cooperation within the framework of the Indian Ocean Rim will be based on respect for the principles of sovereign equality, territorial integrity, political independence, non-interference in internal affairs, peaceful co-existence and mutual benefit;

(ii) The Association will be open to all sovereign States of the Indian Ocean Rim which subscribe to the principles and objectives of the Charter and are willing to undertake commitments under the Charter;

(iii) Decision on all matters and issues and at all levels will be taken on the basis of consensus;

(iv) Bilateral and other issues likely to generate controversy and be an impediment to regional cooperation efforts will be excluded from deliberations;

(v) Cooperation within the Association is without prejudice to rights and obligations entered into by Member States within the framework of other economic and trade cooperation arrangements and will not automatically apply to Member States of the Association. It will not be a substitute for, but seek to reinforce, be complementary to and consistent with their bilateral, plurilateral and multilateral obligations;

(vi) Within the framework of the Association, Member States will pursue adequate measures to promote the achievement of its objective, and will not take any action likely to prejudice its objectives and activities;

(vii) The Work Programmes of the Association will be undertaken by Member States on a voluntary basis.

Objectives

3. The objectives of the association will be :

(i) To promote the sustained growth and balanced development of the region and of the Member States, and to create common ground for regional economic cooperation;

(ii) To focus on those areas of economic cooperation which provide maximum opportunities to develop shared interests and reap mutual benefits. Towards this end, to formulate and implement: projects for economic cooperation relating to trade facilitation, promotion and liberalization; promotion of foreign investment, scientific and technological exchanges, and tourism, movement of natural persons and service providers on a non-discriminatory basis; and development of infrastructure and human resources, as laid down in the Work Programmes of the Association;

(iii) To identify other areas of cooperation as may be mutually agreed;

(iv) Towards promoting liberalisation, to remove impediments to, and lower barriers towards, freer and enhanced flow of goods, services, investment and technology within the region;

(v) To explore all possibilities and avenues for trade liberalisation with a view to augmenting and diversifying trade flows among Member States;

(vi) To encourage close interaction of trade and industry, academic institutions, scholars and the peoples of the Member States without any discrimination among Member States and without prejudice to obligations under other regional economic and trade cooperation arrangements;

(vii) To strengthen cooperation and dialogue among Member States in international fora on global economic issues, and where desirable to develop shared strategies and take common positions in the international fora on issues of mutual interest; and

(viii) To promote cooperation in development of human resources, particularly through closer linkages among training institutions, universities and other specialized institutions of the Member States.

Membership

4. All sovereign States of the Indian Ocean Rim are eligible for membership. To become members, States must adhere to the principles and objectives enshrined in the Charter of the Association. Expansion of membership of the Association will be decided by Member States.

Institutional Mechanism

5. There will be Council of Ministers of the Association. The Council will meet once in two years, or more often as mutually decided, for formulation of policies, review of progress of cooperation, decisions on new areas of cooperation, establishment of additional mechanisms as deemed necessary, and decisions on other matters of general interest.

6. There will be a Committee of Senior Officials of the Association composed of government officials of Member States. It will meet as often as mutually decided. It will review implementation of the decisions taken by the Council of Ministers; and in cooperation with the Indian Ocean Rim business Forum (IORBF) and the Indian Ocean Rim Academic Group (IORAG) establish priorities of economic cooperation, develop, monitor and coordinate Work Programmes, and mobilise resources for financing of Work Programmes. The Committee will submit periodic reports to the Council of Ministers, and refer, as and when necessary, policy matters for the Council's decision.

7. There will be a Secretariat of the Association to coordinate, service and monitor the implementation of policy decisions and Work Programmes as laid down.

National Focal Points

8. Each Member State of the Association will set up a tripartite National Focal Point for Indian Ocean Rim cooperation to co-ordinate and advance implementation of its activities and achievement of its objectives.

Indian Ocean Rim Business Forum (IORBF) and Indian Ocean Rim Academic Group (Iorag)

9. The Association includes bodies known as the Indian Ocean Rim Business Forum (IORBF) and the Indian Ocean Rim Academic Group (IORAG) in accordance with the tripartite nature of the Association. They may meet together with the Council of Ministers and the Committee of Senior Officials as mutually decided. They may also meet as and when they deem it necessary. They will interact with the Committee of senior officials and the Secretariat in the consideration, formulation and implementation of the policies and Work Programmes of the Association. The IORBF and the IORAG may draw upon other non-governmental regional business and academic networks, as necessary.

Financial Arrangements

10. Each Member State will contribute to the finances of the Association as decided. Adequate arrangements will be made by participating Member States for providing finances for implementing the Work Programmes. This will not exclude external sources of financing where appropriate.

The Member States will endeavor to promote the spirit of economic cooperation enshrined in the Charter of the Association.

Appendix G

Naval capacities of India, Pakistan and China

A. Indian Navy

Personnel	55000
Submarines	16
Aircraft Carrier	1
Destroyers	8
Frigates	12
Corvettes	25
Fast Attack Craft-Missile	2
Fleet Tankers	3
Maritime Patrol Aircraft	33

B. Pakistani Navy

Personnel	22,000
Submarines	7
Aircraft Carrier	0
Destroyers	3
Frigates	8
Corvettes	0

Fast Attack Craft-Missile	9
Fleet Tankers	1
Maritime Patrol Aircraft	4

C. Chinese Navy

Personnel	2,68,000
Submarines	66
Aircraft Carrier	0
Destroyers	22
Frigates	36
Corvettes	20
Fast Attack Craft-Missile	83
Fleet Tankers	6
Maritime Patrol Aircraft	12

Source: India Today, May 12, 2003

Bibliograply

A. Books

1. Adie, WAC- *Oil Politics and Sea Power; The Indian Ocean Vortex*, Cranse Hussale and Company, New York, 1975.
2. Amiri, Abbas (ed)- *The Persian Gulf and Indian Ocean in International Politics*, Tehran, 1975.
3. Ball, Desmond and Mack Andrew (ed.) - *Arms Control and the Indian Ocean*, Australian National University, Sydney, 1987.
4. Ballard, G.A. - *Rulers of the Indian Ocean*, Houghton Mifflin Company, London, 1938.
5. Bannerji, B.N. - *Indian Ocean: A Whirlpool of unrest, Paribus*, New Delhi, 1984.
6. Bezboruah, Monoranjan - *US Strategy in the Indian Ocean: International Response*, Prager, New York, USA, 1977.
7. Bhasin, V.K. - *Super Power rivalry in the Indian Ocean*, S. Chand and Company Ltd., New Delhi, 1981.
8. Bhatt, Anita - *Indian Ocean Foreign Relation in 1980's. The Strategic Role of Indian Ocean in World Politics (The Case of Diego Garcia)* Delhi, Ajanta, 1992.
9. Borsa, Giorgio (ed.) - Trade and Politics in the Indian Ocean; Historical and Contemporary Perspectives, Manohar, New Delhi 1990.
10. Bowman, Larry and Clark ,Ian - *Indian Ocean Global Politics*, Defence Publications, Bombay, 1985.
11. Braun, Dieter - *The Indian Ocean: Region of Conflict or Zone of Peace*? Oxford University Press, New Delhi,1983.

12. Burke, W.T. - Towards a Better Use of the Ocean : Contemporary Legal Problems in Ocean Development, Almquist and Wikseell, Stockholm, 1969.

13. Chandra Satish, B. Arunachalam, V. Suryanarayan (ed) - *The Indian Ocean and Its Islands: Strategic, Scientific and Historical Perspectives, Sage,* New Delhi, 1993.

14. Chandra, *Satish-Indian Ocean: Explorations in History, Commerce and Politics,* Sage, New Delhi, 1987.

15. Chopra, Maharaj K. - India and the Indian Ocean; New Horizons, Sterling, New Delhi, 1982.

16. Cottrell - Burrell - *Indian Ocean : Its Political, Economic and Military Importance,* Prager, USA, 1972.

17. Cubitt, Gerald - Islands of the Indian Ocean; Cassell and Co. London, 1977.

18. Dasgupta, Ashinand Pearson, MN (ed.) - *India and the Indian Ocean 1500-1800,* Oxford University Press, Calcutta, 1987.

19. Dowdy William L. and Trood - Indian Ocean: Perspectives on a Strategic Arena, Himalaya, New Delhi, 1987.

20. Gupta, Ranjan - *Indian Ocean: A Political Geography,* Marwah, New Delhi, 1979.

21. Gyatso, Geshe Kelsang – Ocean of the Nector, Motilal Banarsidas, Delhi, 1999.

22. Hourani G.J. - Arab Sea Faring in the Indian Ocean in Ancient and Early Medieval Times - Princeton University Press, 1951.

23. Jackson, Ashley - War and Empire in Mauritius and the Indian Ocean, Palgrave, London, 2001

24. Jawatkar, K.S. - *Diego Garcia in International Diplomacy,* Popular Prakashan, Bombay, 1983.

25. Kakkar, A.N. - *Indian Ocean, Proceeding of an International Seminar,* New Book House, Allahabad, 1987.

26. Kapur, Ashok - *The Indian Ocean Region and International Power Politics*, Prager, USA, 1983.

27. Kaul, T.N. - *India, China and Indo-China*, Lancer, New Delhi, 1987.

28. Kaushika, Devendra - *Indian Ocean Towards a Peace Zone*, Vikas, Delhi, 1972.

29. Kaushika, Devendra - *Perspectives of Security in Indian Ocean Region*, Allied, New Delhi, 1987.

30. Kaushika, Devendra - *The Indian Ocean: A Strategic Dimension*, Vikas, New Delhi, 1983.

31. Khan, Rahmatulla - *Indian Ocean Fisheries: The 200 Mile Economic Zone*, New Delhi, Ankur, 1977.

32. Kohli, S.N. - *The Indian Ocean and India's Maritime Security*, United Service Institute of India, New Delhi, 1981.

33. Kohli, S.N. - *Sea Power and the Indian Ocean with Special Reference to India*, Tata McGraw Hill Publishing Company Ltd., New Delhi, 1978.

34. Krutshikh, Andri - *US Policies in the Indian Ocean*, Progress, Moscow, 1984.

35. Kumar, Kamal - Indian Ocean as a Zone of Peace - APH, New Delhi, 2000.

36. Lombard, Denys and Aubin, Jean (ed.) - Asian Merchants and Business in the Indian Ocean and the China Sea, Oxford University Press, New Delhi, 2000.

37. Mazeed, Akhtar (ed.) - *Indian Ocean: Conflict and Regional Cooperation*, ABC, New Delhi, 1986.

38. McPherson Kenneth - The Indian Ocean; A History of People and the Sea, Oxford University Press, New Delhi, 1993.

39. McPherson, Kenneth - *The Indian Ocean, A History of People and the Sea*, Oxford, New Delhi, 1995.

40. Melkote, Rama S. (ed.) - *Indian Ocean : Issues for Peace*, Manohar, New Delhi, 1995.

41. Miller, T.B. - *The Indian and Pacific Oceans, Some strategic Considerations*, London, 1969.

42. Misra, K.P. - *Quest for an International Order in the Indian Ocean*, Allied Publishers Pvt. Ltd., New Delhi, 1977.

43. Misra, Raj Narain - *Indian Ocean and India's Security*, Mittal, Delhi 1986.

44. Mohan C. Raja and Others - India Ocean and IJS - Soviet Detente, Patriot, New Delhi, 1991.

45. Mukherjee, Rudrangshu and Subramaniam, Lakshmi (ed) - Politics and Trade in the Indian Ocean World, Oxford University Press, Oxford, 1999.

46. Nambiar, O.K. - Our Sea faring in the Indian Ocean, Jeevan, Bangalore, 1975.

47. Namboodari, P.K.S. and Anand, J.P. - *Intervention in the Indian Ocean*, ABC, New Delhi, 1982.

48. Nitze, Paul H (etc.) - Securing the Seas, The Soviet Naval Challenge and Western Alliance Options, Bouldel, Colorado, Westview, 1979.

49. Pannikkar, K.M. - *India and Indian Ocean*, George Allen and Unwin, Bombay, 1971.

50. Parkin, David and Barnes, Ruth (ed) – Ships and the Development of Maritime Technology in the Indian Ocean - Routledge Curzon, London, 2002.

51. Patra, Saral (Ed.) - *Indian Ocean and Great Powers*, Sterling, New Delhi, 1979.

52. Patrick, Wall- *The Indian Ocean and threat to the West*, Stacey International, London, 1975.

53. Philip Allen - *Security and Nationalism in the Indian Ocean*, Allen and Unwin, London, 1971.

54. Poulose, T.T. (ed.) - *Indian Ocean Power Rivalry*, Young Asia, New Delhi, 1974.

55. Prabha Roy, Himanshu (ed) - Archeology of Sea Faring; The Indian Ocean in the Ancient Period, Pragati, Delhi, 1999.

56. Qasim, S.Z. (ed) - India Ocean in the 21st Century; Linkages and Networking, Sai, New Delhi, 2000.

57. Qasim, S.Z .- Indian Ocean : Images and Realities, Oxford and IBH, New Delhi, 1999.

58. Rahul, Roy Chaudhary - *Sea Power and Indian Security*, Brasey's, London.

59. Rais Rasul, B. - *Indian Ocean and the Super Power: Economic, Political and Strategic Perspectives*, London Cromm Helm, London, 1986.

60. Rajamohan, C & Singh, K.R. etc. (ed.) - *Indian Ocean and US Soviet detente*, Patriot, New Delhi, 1991.

61. Rama, Rao, & Pattabhi, P. - *Diego Garcia Towards a Zone of Peace*, Sterling, New Delhi, 1985.

62. Rao, T.S.S. and Griffiths, Roy C. – Understanding the Indian Ocean: Perspectives on Oceanography, UNESCO, Paris. 1998.

63. Remnek, Richard B. – *The Soviet-naval presence in the Indian Ocean and Western Security in US Strategic interests in the Gulf Region*, (ed. by W.M. Jalson, Boulder), Westviao Press, 1987.

64. Roonwal, G.S.- *Indian Ocean: Exploitable Mineral and Petroleum Resources*, Naroso, New Delhi, 1986.

65. Roy, H.P. and Salles, J.F. - Tradition and Archeology; Early Maritime Contacts in the Indian Ocean, Manohar, Delhi, 2000.

66. Roy, Mihir K. – War in the Indian Ocean, Lancer, New Delhi, 1995.

67. Sadiq, Ali Shanti and Ramchandani, R.R. (ed.) – *India and the Western Indian Ocean States*, Allied, New Delhi, 1981.

68. Siddiquin, M.A.H. – India in the Indian Ocean: A Geopolitical Study, Rawat, Jaipur, 1997.

69. Sindhu, K.S. - *Indian Ocean: A Zone of Peace*, Harnam, New Delhi, 1983.

70. Singh, Bhupinder – *Indian Ocean and Regional Security*, BC Publishers, Patiala, 1983.

71. Singh, K.R. – *Indian Ocean: Big Powers presence, local response*, Manohar, New Delhi, 1977.

72. Singh, Rajendra K. – *Politics of the Indian Ocean*, Thomson, Delhi, 1974.

73. Singh, Ranbir - Mauritius; The Key to the Indian Ocean, Arnold Heinemann, New Delhi, 1980.

74. Sridharan, K. (Real Admiral AVSM Retd.) – *A Maritime History of India, Ministry of Information and Broadcasting*, Govt. of India, Oxford, 1989, New Delhi, 1982.

75. Steinberg, Philip E. - Social Construction of the Ocean, Cambridge University Press, Cambridge, 2001.

76. Subramanyam, K. and Selig, A. Harrison - *Sea Power Rivalry in the Indian Ocean, Indian and American Perspectives*, Oxford, 1989.

77. Taraz Fawaz, Leila and Bayly C.A. (ed.) Modernity and Culture from the Mediterranean to the Indian Ocean, Columbia University Press, New York, 2001.

78. Toussaint, Auguste - *History of the Indian Ocean*, Routledge and Kegan, London, 1966.

79. Towel, Philip - *Naval Powers in the Indian Ocean: Threats, Bluffs and Fantasies*, Canberra, 1979.

80. Vaidya, K.B. - *The Naval Defence of India*, Tharker and Company, Bombay, 1949.

81. Vali, Ference Albert - Politics of the Indian Ocean Region: The Balance of Power, Free Press, New York, 1976.

82. Vibhakar, Jagdish - Afro -Asian Security and Indian Ocean, Sterling, New Delhi, 1974.

83. Villers, Allan – *The Indian Ocean*, Museum Press, London, 1952.

84. Von Der Borch and Chris C. (ed) – Synthesis of Deep Sea Drilling Results in the Indian Ocean, Elsevier, Amsterdam, 1978.

85. Wall, Patrick (Ed.) – *The Indian Ocean and the Threat to the West*, Stacey International, London, 1975.

86. Walsh Don (ed) - The Law of the Sea, Issues in Ocean Resource Management, Prager, New York, 1977.

87. Wenk, Edward - The Politics of the Ocean, University of Washington Press, Seattle, 1979.

88. Zeitzschel, Bernt (ed) - Biology of the Indian Ocean, Chapman, London, 1973.

B. Articles:

1. *A Framework to beat transnational terror*, The Straits Times, 21 Jul. 2004.

2. *A Lax attitude can land us in deep water*, The Straits Times, 22 May 2004.

3. Arbuckle (Tammy) - *Scourge of Piracy Returns to Southeast Asia*. International Defence Review 29, Aug. 1996; pp 26-29.

4. Arizala (Rodolfo A) - *Shall we implement the United Nations Convention on the Law of the Sea (UNCLOS)?* Foreign Relations Journal (11)2, June. 1996; pp 51-57.

5. Ball (Desmond and Bateman Sam) - *An Australian Perspective on Maritime CSBMs in the Asia-Pacific region*, Canberra; Research School of Pacific Studies, Australian National University, 1991. pp 30.

6. Beckman (Robert C.) *Issues of Public International Law Relating to Piracy and Armed Robbery Against Ships in*

the Malacca and Singapore Straits. Singapore Journal of International and Comparative Law (3), 2, 1999, pp 512-523.

7. Bergin (Anthony) - *New Developments in the Law of the Sea: The Changing Context of Naval Operations.* Asian Defence Journal, Jan. 1992; pp 34-42.
8. Boxhall (Peter) - Arabian Seafarers in the Indian Ocean, *Asian Affairs* (20) October 1989, pp. 287-295.
9. Boxhall (Peter) - Portuguese Sea Farers in the Indian Ocean, *Asian Affairs,* London (23) Oct. 1992, Pp. 322-330.
10. Burlatskiy (Freed) - *The Navies of the ASEAN states.* Asian Defence Journal, Sep. 1990; pp. 44-46.
11. Chanda (Nayan) - *Security: Foot in the Water. Far Eastern Economic Review,* (163) 10, 9 Mar. 2000; pp. 28-29.
12. *Chasing pirates.* Far Eastern Economic Review (167) 24, 17 Jun. 2004, p 8.
13. Cheema (Pervaiz Iqbal) - *Indian naval buildup and Southeast Asian security: a Pakistani view,* Contemporary Southeast Asia (13), 1 Jun. 1991; p 86-102.
14. Da Cunha (Derek) *ASEAN Naval Power in the New Millennium.* In Sea Power in the New Century: Maritime Operations in the Asia-Pacific Beyond 2000, Australian Defence Studies Centre, Canberra: 1998, pp. 73-83.
15. De Silva (Chandra Richard) - Indian Ocean but not African Sea : The Erasure of East African commerce from History, *Journal of Black Studies* (29) 5, May 1999, pp. 684-694.
16. Djalal (Hasjim) - *Evolution in the Law of the Sea: From High Seas Regime to Exclusive Economic Zone to Cooperation.* The Indonesian Quarterly (21), 2, 2nd Qtr. 1993; pp 214-228.
17. —. *The Law of the Sea after UNCLOS: Implication for the South China Seas Dispute.* Kuala Lumpur: Malaysian Institute of Maritime Affair, No. 7, 1995.

18. Djalal (Hasjim) - *Piracy and the Challenges of Cooperative Security and Enforcement Policy,* Indonesia Quarterly (30), 2, 2002; pp 106-116.

19. Drifte (Reinhard) - *Japan's security policy and Southeast Asia.* Contemporary Southeast Asia (12) 3, Dec. 1990; pp 186-197.

20. Ellen (Eric) - *A Look into Asian piracy.* Asian Defence Journal, Sep. 1992; pp. 19-22.

21. Emmers (Ralf) - *Non-traditional Security in the Asia-Pacific - The Dynamics of securitisation.* Eastern Universities Press, Singapore, p 84.

22. Francisco, (John). *Ever Ready to Combat Terrorist Threat.* The Shipping Times, 6 May 2003.

23. Gilley (Bruce) - *How will Asia cope with a wounded United States.* Far Eastern Economic Review (164) 37, Sep. 20,2001; p. 19.

24. *Going for the jugular - Shipping in South-East Asia.* The Economist, 12 Jun. 2004.

25. Haubert (Jean) - The Indian Ocean Creole Island : Geo Politics and Decolonization *The Journal of Modern African Studies* (30) Sep. 1992, pp. 465-484.

26. *Industry Must be More Vigilant Against Terrorist Attacks,* The Shipping Times, 16 Oct. 2002.

27. *Japan Offers Counter-Piracy Programme,* The Jakarta Post, 5 Apr. 2000.

28. Juwana (Hikmahanto) - *Japan's defence conception and its implications for Southeast Asia,* The Indonesian Quarterly (21) 4, 4th Qtr. 1993; pp. 483-494.

29. Kerr (Pauline) - *Maritime Security in the 1990s; Achievements and Prospects.* In a peaceful ocean? Maritime security in the Pacific in the post-cold war era. St Leonards, NW, Australia: Allen & Unwin, in association with the Dept. of International Relations, the Peace Research Centre,

RSPasS, ANU, and the Institute of Strategic and International Studies, 1993, pp. 186-202.

30. Laroya (Leopoldo V). *Piracy in Southeast Asia: Examining the Present and Revisiting the Problems of Definition, Prevention, Response and Prosecution,* Thesis, World Maritime University, 2000.

31. Linter (Bertil) - Burma Road : China's Economic Press Southward Worries Neighbours, *Far Eastern Economic Review*, (160) Nov. 6, 1997, pp. 16-17.

32. *Liss (Carolin) - Maritime Piracy in Southeast Asia*. Southeast Asian Affairs 2003. pp 52-68.

33. Mack (Andrew) - *ASEAN maritime insecurity: contingency planning in an uncertain world*, International Defence Review, 1995; pp 58-65.

34. Mak (J. N.) and Hamzah (B.A.) - *The External maritime dimension of ASEAN security.* Journal of Strategic Studies (18) 3, Sep. 1995, pp 123-146.

35. *Malacca straits needs US support,* Business Times, Singapore, 10 Apr. 2004.

36. *Maritime plan aims to make the region's waters secure,* The Straits Times, 26 Apr. 2004.

37. *Maritime security: running short on time... and money. (Maritime & Port Security).* Marine Log, 1 Jun. 2003.

38. *Maritime terrorism phase next*? The Washington Times, 20 Oct. 2002.

39. Mcbeth (John) - Murky Waters: Security Concerns hamper Oceanographic Research, *Far Eastern Economic Review* (158) 30, 1995, pp. 29-30.

40. McCawley, (Tom) - Sea of trouble. Far Eastern Economic Review (167), 21, 27 May 2004; pp 50-52.

41. *Mills (Greg) Maritime policy for developing nations.* South African Institute of International Affairs, Johannesburg; 1995, p.299.

42. *More work needs to be done to improve maritime safety.* Business World, 9 Sep. 2003.

43. *Most ships to US meet security test, ports a concern-HLS.* Dow Jones Energy Service, 2 Jul. 2004.

44. *Nothing Jolly about the Pirates Bringing Terror to the High Seas,* Scotland on Sunday, 14 Jul. 2002.

45. Olson (Theodore) - *Maritime Strategy and the new law of the sea : Losers and Gainers: with Focus on Southeast Asia.* : Centre for International and Strategic Studies, York University, No. 17, 1996. p.16

46. Pane (S. Zuhdi) - *The implementation of UNO convention on the Law of the sea 1982.* Telstra 41, Jul - Aug 1996; pp 45-51.

47. *Piracy and Maritime Terror in Southeast Asia.* Strategic Comments 10, 6 Jul. 2004.

48. *Piracy in South-East Asia; Obstacles to Security Cooperation.* Strategic Comments (6), 5, Jun. 2000.

49. *Piracy in Southeast Asian waters.* Pointer (18) 3 Jul. / Sep. 1992; pp. 154-159.

50. *Piracy is deadlier than ever,* United States Naval Institute; Proceedings, 1 Jan. 2000.

51. Roy-Chaudhury (Rahul) - *Maritime security: on the growing importance of the Indian Ocean.* Seminar New Delhi; 448, Dec. 1996.

52. *Rush to Comply with New Rules May Affect Maritime Security.* The Straits Times, 30 June. 2004.

53. *Sea Terror Threat Stirs Asia.* South China Morning Post, 16 May 2004.

54. *Seaborne Nuclear Attack a Chilling Reality.* The Straits Times, 13 Jun. 2004.

55. Sengupta (Prasun K.) *Japan Conducts First Bilateral Anti-Piracy Exercises in East Asia,* Asian Defence Journal, Dec. 2000; pp. 10-11.

56. ____. *Piracy Incidents on the Rise in Southeast Asia*, Asian Defence and Diplomacy. (3) 4, Apr. 1997; pp 65-66.

57. *Shipowners can take steps against pirate attacks*, The Shipping Time, 5 Feb. 2003.

58. *Shots in the dark: Pirates, Pillage and Peter Blake*. Australian Financial Review, 6 Jul. 2002.

59. *Singapore confronts Fear of Seaborne Terror*. Reuters News, 8 Jan. 2003.

60. Singh (Jasjit) ed. - *Maritime security*, Institute for Defence Studies and Analyses, 1993. New Delhi, p. 182.

61. _____. *Reshaping Asian security*, Knowledge World with Institute for Defence Studies and Analyses, 2001; New Delhi: p. 365.

62. *S'pore gears up to face new security threats*, The Straits Times, 29 Jul. 2004.

63. *Taking up the challenge*, The Shipping Times, 28 Jan. 2003.

64. Tan (Tony), *Policing the sea is a job for everyone*, The Straits Times, 3 Jun. 2003.

65. *Terror on the seas*, Business Times, Singapore, 20 April 2004.

66. *Terror threat Puts East Asia in a Spin*, Lloyd's List no. 58699, 13 Jul. 2004;:1.

67. *Terrorists or pirates ? The line gets thinner*, The Straits Times, 2 Jan. 2004

68. *Terror-piracy nexus - IMO seeks global action*, The Shipping Times, 21 May 2004.

69. *The Piracy menace*. Seaways, Jul. 2004; pp. 3-4.

70. Tow (William T., et al, eds.) *Asia's emerging regional order: reconciling traditional and human security*. United Nations University Press, Tokyo; New York: 2000 p. 342.

71. *U.S. Interest in Malacca Strait*, Korea Herald, 8 Jul. 2004.

72. *Unity is security for Asian ports*, Lloyd's List, 24 Oct. 2002.

Index